# Show Training for
# You and Your Dog

# SHOW TRAINING FOR YOU AND YOUR DOG

JULIETTE CUNLIFFE

**POPULAR DOGS**
London Sydney Auckland Johannesburg

Popular Dogs Publishing Co. Ltd

An imprint of the Random Century Group
20 Vauxhall Bridge Road, London SW1V 2SA

Random Century Australia (Pty) Ltd
20 Alfred Street, Milsons Point,
Sydney, NSW 2061

Random Century New Zealand Limited
191 Archers Road, PO Box 40–086, Glenfield,
Auckland 10

Century Hutchinson South Africa (Pty) Ltd
PO Box 337, Bergvlei 2012, South Africa

First published 1991
Set in Baskerville by Speedset Ltd, Ellesmere Port

Printed and bound in Great Britain by
Clays Ltd, St. Ives PLC
a4British Library Cataloguing in Publication Data
Cunliffe, Juliette
Show training for you and your dog.
1. Livestock : Dogs. Showing
I. Title   II. Series
636.70888

ISBN 0 09 174559 4

**All photographs by Carol Ann Johnson,
except pages 13, 15, 18 and 19**

# Contents

## *Acknowledgements*

Grateful thanks to the Kennel Club for having permitted inclusion of some of its rules and to its library staff for their usual much-valued assistance.

My thanks must, of course, go also to Carol Ann Johnson for the many patient hours she spent taking photographs at shows.

Dedicated to my father who,
though he never understood my obsession
with dogs, loved them all the same.

# Author's preface

Writing a book with a title such as this makes one think – my goodness, there was a lot to learn in those early days! Those of us who have been exhibiting dogs for many years take so much for granted and do so much automatically; almost certainly, if you enjoy the 'dog game' and remain an enthusiastic exhibitor, you, too, will get to know exactly how to fill in a show schedule and in which classes to enter your dog without having to give the matter much thought. You will also have just the right equipment for your dog and will know how to present your exhibit to perfection. But all this takes time and most people make many expensive errors along the way. I hope that this book will help you to speed up the process so that you get the best out of your dog and give yourself every opportunity to win, without making fundamental mistakes which can be avoided – if you know what to avoid!

I have endeavoured to make things as explicit as possible and have included a couple of useful glossaries in the last chapter to help you come to terms with some of the words and expressions used in canine circles which can, to the outsider or relative newcomer, be somewhat misleading.

I hope all bitch owners will forgive me for having referred to dogs of the masculine sex throughout the text, unless I refer specifically to bitches. Naturally, for the most part what I have to say concerns both sexes. Likewise, I hope that if any male judges peruse this book they will not mind my having mentioned primarily female judges in the text. This, I promise you, has been done simply to avoid confusion.

Lastly, let me say that I hope I have made it clear that almost every breed is handled, prepared and exhibited in a slightly different way and it goes without saying that you will want to learn as much as possible about every aspect of your own particular breed. For these reasons it is imperative that you also have access to a good book which is specific to the breed you have chosen to exhibit. If the breed publication you have selected gives sound advice, you should find that with that book and this one you have all the information you require to set you and your dog on the road towards a successful show career.

# Introduction

## The history of dog shows

The first time we think about taking up the sport of dog showing it seems new and exciting, and so it is. But before you get too involved, stop for a moment to think about its history for, in doing so, you will understand a little more about how the sport has developed. As a result of your greater understanding you will almost certainly get more enjoyment out of your new-found hobby.

Events which can loosely be described as dog shows have undoubtedly been taking place for thousands of years, and certainly by the eighteenth century there were shows which would have been remotely familiar to exhibitors today. As a way of keeping contact with fellow huntsmen outside the hunting season, John Warde, who hunted a pack of hounds in Kent, held hound shows during the summer months. The first of these took place in 1776. The agricultural shows of the late eighteenth century also included dog sections, and by then the value of dogs as companions had also become greatly appreciated by towns-folk. It has been estimated that as many as 25 per cent of households possessed a dog, whereas today the estimate is only about half that number in Britain. There was an increasing change in attitudes towards some of the more brutal sports involving dogs, and by the end of the eighteenth century a growing sentiment of humanity had led to protests against bull-baiting. By 1801 Joseph Strutt in *Sports and Pastimes* said, 'Bull and bear baiting is not encouraged by persons of rank and opulence in the present day, and when practised, which rarely happens, it is attended by only the lowest and most despicable of people.' Clearly opinion was changing, but none the less in 1802 a Bill to abolish bull-baiting was thrown out of the House of Commons.

Finally, in 1835, an Act was passed to abolish the bloodthirsty pursuits of bull-baiting, cock-fighting, dog-fighting and 'other cruel sports'.

Around the same time more delicate canine sports were coming into fashion. In 1834 a show was held for '9lb spaniels', and the prize was a silver cream jug. The event took place in a public house and it was indeed in such drinking houses that the sport of dog showing began; in many cases this merely represented a change from former gatherings around the dog-pit. Dog clubs then evolved, the venues for meetings being almost invariably public houses, and it was reported in the press of the time that the bars were often 'crowded with men of every grade of society'. One such club incorporated a rule that each member was expected to take along a dog, either for show or for sale, so that a good 'show night' was ensured.

Although shows of the type described thrived in both urban and rural localities during the early part of the nineteenth century, it was not until the advent of railway travel that those involved in 'The Fancy' were able to travel to participate in the sport of which they were becoming increasingly fond. That which has become known as the 'very first dog show' was held in the New Corn Exchange at Newcastle-on-Tyne on 28 and 29 June 1859. Thanks to the advent of the railway, exhibitors came from far afield and at least one of the judges had travelled all the way from London.

The dog show was held as part of a well-established poultry show, and breed competition was restricted to Pointers and Setters, although there were other dogs and puppies at the event for the purposes of exhibition. Arrangements for the show were highly praised, the dogs being chained and protected by barriers so that they could neither injure nor alarm visitors to the show. Twenty-three Pointers were entered, having travelled from 'all parts of the kingdom' including Manchester, Huddersfield and Lancaster, and the best was awarded one of Pape's celebrated double-barrelled guns worth between £15 and £20. Thirty-six competed in the Setter classes and again the lucky first-prize-winner became the proud owner of a double-barrelled gun. One of the judges was Mr J.H. Walsh, then editor of *The Field* and now best known for his literary works under the guise of 'Stonehenge'. He was to become one of the organisers of the next show, which took place in Birmingham later that year and which led to the formation of the Birmingham Dog Show Society. Indeed,

*A dog show at the Agricultural Hall, Islington, circa 1863*

Birmingham was very much a stronghold of the dog fancy and by 1902 was praised for having held a dog show there for forty-three consecutive years; it is doubtful that any town in the whole world could show such a record of consistency.

As the nineteenth century progressed, the popularity of shows increased; in 1862 a show at the New Agricultural Hall at Islington in London drew an entry of 803, while in May 1863 the event at Islington, entitled the 'First Great International Dog Show', mustered an entry of 1678, and as many of the entries comprised several dogs it was estimated that there were probably over 2000 dogs in the hall. A show in March of that same year was reported in detail in *The Field* and I make no excuse for quoting at some length, for the content of the report was to have substantial bearing on shows of the future. As you, the reader, become increasingly familiar with dog showing in this present day and age, you will appreciate this extract more and more. The show was called 'The First Annual Grand National Exhibition of Sporting and Other Dogs' and was held in Chelsea under the guidance of Mr E.T. Smith who managed to draw an entry of 1214 dogs at his show. But drawing an entry was not all that was needed, as we shall see.

A great man struggling under difficulties is said to be one of the grandest sights in creation; and if so the British public must have been highly favoured during the past week for while it is universally admitted that Mr E.T. Smith is a great man (in his way), it is patent to all who have witnessed his labours that he has been overwhelmed by the difficulties of the task which he has undertaken. No doubt, in his comprehensive mind it appeared simple enough to collect together, first a lot of dogs to be seen, and then a mass of spectators to see them; but he had overlooked the fact that these animals must be provided for in a way that should at once conduce to their health as well as to the instruction and gratification of his guests. To effect these objects there must be some knowledge of the habits of the dog, as well as of the varieties; but in both these departments of natural history Mr Smith and his subordinates seem to be utterly deficient. We should have imagined that no Englishman could be ignorant of the fact that dogs require constant access to water when in confinement . . . an earthen pan might easily have been replenished from the fountain which formed a veritable torture of Tantalus in the middle of the building. We can only attribute [this omission] to gross ignorance of the habits of the dog. This opinion is confirmed by the general arrangements, or rather by the absolute want of them, exhibited throughout the show. For instance, instead of the intending exhibitors being furnished, as is usually the case, with numbered tickets, to be tied to the collars of the dogs, each dog was labelled with the name and address of the owner and thus the judges could not avoid knowing the proprietors of the animals they were selecting for prizes. . . .

A worse omission, however, than the absence of water is the crowding of the dogs, without any proper division between them. The Hall itself is capable of properly accommodating 600 dogs on the ground but this number can only be safely arranged there by separating each dog in the middle tiers from his fellows by wooden partitions. Not only has Mr Smith dispensed with partitions altogether between the dogs in each row, but he has introduced an open wire fence between the rows themselves, thus completely preventing the poor dogs from retreating into a quiet corner in any one direction. In front they have the spectators to guard against, close on each side is an animal of the same variety of the species canis, while behind them is another of a separate class, who can express his disgust and contempt in the way most galling to the feelings of the poor brutes, as well as physically disagreeable to their skins . . . the veterinary surgeon, who has been appointed since the commencement of the show, has been in constant requisition . . . .

. . . the new wing, specially built for the toy and pet dogs, certainly does no credit to the supervision of Messrs Brown and Gilbert, who have long been announced as taking this department under their fostering care, for, from the nature of its roof (of glass), it is sure to be either too warm or too cold. Indeed, when we entered it on Monday, under a glaring sun, it was hot enough to produce dehydration, especially in the absence of water. . . . Beyond this every arrangement was as bad as possible. To find any particular specimen was a long task, and, in many cases, when the proper number was reached, either the animal indicated in the catalogue was absent, or it was misplaced in the wrong class, or it did not correspond at all with the description. . . .

*Prize winning dogs at the National Dog Show, Islington, circa 1863*

Among the foreign dogs confusion reigned pre-eminently; five or six had no numbers attached, and a lot of puppies occupied the bench allotted to No. 1195, which is described in the catalogue as 'Wolf, brought from Crimea'. . . . The visitors on the first day could gain no information as to the prizes; for, though the judges had nearly completed their labours on Saturday, no prize list was published. . . . A general opinion was expressed that the 'screw was being applied' to change the verdicts of the judges in certain cases, but this of course was only a canard, although we do happen to know that the statement of a judge as to his selection in one class, made to us on Monday, did not correspond with the prize list as it appeared the following day. He may have made a mistake, but it is very curious if it was so, as we had a long discussion on the merits of the very animals concerned.

This long and highly critical report, very probably written by J.H. Walsh, the gentleman we know as 'Stonehenge', had a great bearing on dog shows of the future and it was evident from the reports given in *The Field* in subsequent years that promoters of shows had already begun to take heed, for they were substantially more careful in making suitable arrangements for their shows.

It was at Islington in 1869 that a show was held with reportedly the best quality of dogs ever seen up to that time. But high entries were found at other shows too, although each was conducted under its own rules and regulations and it has to be said that some undesirable practices undoubtedly took place. Various local attempts were made to apply reform, and local clubs and societies were formed but their jurisdiction was limited and in consequence they lacked harmony in their policies. Financial difficulties caused problems and people became increasingly cautious, but some success in other respects acted as a spur for the future.

## The beginning of the Kennel Club

Each new show involved the formation of a new committee, and what with the lack of permanent staff and permanent funds Mr Shirley, who had begun exhibiting dogs in 1870 and had been involved also in the organisation of some shows, decided to set himself the task of forming a permanent body which was to become the Kennel Club. It is hard to believe that the Kennel Club we know so well today as a large and highly professional organisation began as a meeting of thirteen people in a small three-roomed flat in April 1873. Later that year they held their first show at Crystal Palace with an entry of 975. The first general meeting of the Kennel Club took place at the Great Western Hotel in Birmingham in December 1874 with the aim of drawing up a fixed code of rules for the better regulation of canine exhibition. Also in that year the Club published its first Stud Book containing the pedigrees of 4027 dogs divided into forty different breeds and varieties, and also giving details of principal winners at shows held prior to its publication. For a young club the Kennel Club took bold steps, shortly afterwards announcing that they would 'disqualify for ever' all dogs exhibited at shows which were not held under Kennel Club rules. Despite the audacity of this statement its message was well received by many, and the Club was supported strongly by owners, exhibitors and the press. The boldness of its actions began to reap rewards.

By 1880 an edict had been passed that all dogs to be exhibited at any show held under Kennel Club rules had to be registered with the Kennel Club under a distinctive name, the purpose of which was to establish, as far as possible, the identity of each dog entered for exhibition. Thus, the club had established itself as a governing authority which effectively levied taxes on dogs for exhibition. As one might expect, there were objections from some, especially the Birmingham Dog Show Society, the committee of which was a very influential body. Eventually, in 1885, two delegates of the Society were allowed to sit on the Kennel Club's Committee, an amicable agreement following a hard-fought battle. The developments made by the Kennel Club followed a natural and logical sequence, and undoubtedly, if it was to remain a successful organisation the steps they had taken were inevitable.

Undoubtedly the Kennel Club justified its existence, and was said to have cleared dog showing of reproach. It popularised the sport and elevated it from venues such as bars and public houses to well-known and fashionable locations such as Crystal Palace, Ranelagh and the Botanical Gardens. Through the Kennel Club people were able to obtain pedigrees for their dogs, and their canine companions were listed on permanent registers; new breeds were encouraged and classifications increased as the years progressed. More than that, it acted as a court of appeal so that wrongs could be set right and dishonesty was made difficult and dangerous. Clearly it established the finest set of dog shows the world had ever seen – indeed, it was said that what the Jockey Club had done for racing the Kennel Club did for dogs.

## Who participated in dog showing?

In the mid nineteenth century the majority of 'dog fanciers', as they were popularly called, were not the elite of society, but the intervention of the Kennel Club brought with it a certain respectability to dog showing and many eminent personages came to take part. The royal family seems always to have had a reputation of fondness for our canine friends, and many of them have taken an active interest in shows. Queen Victoria herself was an exhibitor, and in 1875 the Prince of Wales became Patron of the Kennel Club, continuing his patronage following accession to the throne as King Edward VII. He was an active breeder and occasional exhibitor of several varieties of dog while Queen Alexandra was identified mostly with Borzois, Basset Hounds, Chows, Skye Terriers, Japanese Spaniels and Pugs. The royal couple regularly visited shows and took great pleasure in going along the benches, often stopping to talk to the dogs which took their fancy and clearly showing that they were not attending simply in a formal capacity but because they enjoyed seeing good and typical specimens. King George V involved himself mainly

*The Non-sporting Champions class at a dog show just before the turn of the century. On the board is the Bulldog, Ch. Silent Duchess (Source:* The New Book of the Dog, *Robert Leighton, 1907)*

with Labradors and Clumber Spaniels, and though the primary concern was that they could do a good day's work, he did occasionally exhibit those of the best quality.

The nobility also played a very active part: Her Grace the Duchess of Newcastle was thought to have done much to raise the tone of dog shows by her personal patronage, while the Countess of Aberdeen was a patron of the Ladies' Kennel Association and had a deep love of Skye Terriers, inherited from her father, Lord Tweedmouth. One of the wonderful things about dog showing was that it brought all classes together, and many a judge commented that he often had specimens from distinguished kennels competing with others belonging to members of the working classes. There was nothing at all, it was said, to stop the latter dogs being the winners. There were, however, times when it would appear that certain exhibitors were favoured, such as when

Queen Victoria wished to exhibit three Pomeranians of a colour not usually shown in England. A special class was provided for her exhibits and two of them were lucky enough to be awarded joint first prize!

Little has changed. Even today, our common love of dogs brings us all together so that whatever the differences in our

*Queen Alexandra and His Majesty King Edward VII were regular visitors to dog shows and gained much pleasure from talking with dogs on their benches. Circa 1902*

personal circumstances we can all indulge in the same sport and in our favourite hobby. The royal family is still involved, too, Her Majesty Queen Elizabeth II being Patron of the Kennel Club while the Duke of Kent, as President, makes a tour of Cruft's each year and chats interestedly with exhibitors.

# Cruft's

Cruft's is perhaps the most famous dog show in the world. It was founded by Charles Cruft who, rather than continue a career in his father's jewellery business, had worked for James Spratt who was then in business in a small way as a vendor of dog biscuits. The young Cruft became Spratt's right-hand man, and the company grew steadily and had become a limited company when Cruft took over as manager of the Show Department. In this capacity he had plenty of opportunity to visit and manage all kinds of shows both in the UK and in Europe. Mr Cruft's association with Spratt's lasted for many years and upon his retirement he came to an arrangement with Spratt's by which he could hold shows on his own account.

The very first Cruft's show was held in 1886 and was for Terriers only with an entry of 570. Cruft was a man with great energy and ability and by 1891 had arranged a lease with the Agricultural Hall at Islington such that the authorities would not allow any other dog show to be held there, thereby ensuring that none of his competitors, including the Kennel Club, was able to make use of the very best venue available in London.

The fact that Cruft received entries from royalty at his shows was considered a great honour and he made use of the royal crown as part of the show's emblem. Royal dogs were, however, benched 'in a roomy kennel apart from the populace' so that visitors and other exhibitors could view them 'to their hearts' content'. It was in 1891 that all breeds were able to participate, bringing in an entry of almost 2500 dogs and advertised as 'the largest and finest collection of dogs ever brought together'. An important innovation introduced by Cruft at this time was a description of the breeds, written by a suitable 'expert' and printed in the catalogue. This was enhanced by engravings and photographs, and even today a Cruft's catalogue still provides this valuable information.

Charles Cruft was always reputed to pay great attention to

judges and none but the very best was ever invited to officiate at his shows. Nor, it was said, did he ever haggle over expenses to get the best, and some of the most prominent judges from Europe, Canada and the USA officiated at his show. By the turn of this century the name of Cruft's was synonymous with dog shows and it was clear that Cruft's shows were financially a great success. This, of course, was at a time when it was possible to make a personal profit from the organisation of dog shows, something the Kennel Club no longer allows.

Three years after Charles Cruft's death in 1939 his wife decided that she no longer wished to run the show which had become so famous, and in order that the name be perpetuated she asked the Kennel Club to take over the organisation. The war years intervened and the first Cruft's show organised by the Kennel Club took place in 1948 at Olympia in London. It proved an immediate success with exhibitors and public alike. In 1979 it was moved to Earl's Court, and it was decided to extend it to a three-day show in 1982; from 1987 it has been spread over four days. Cruft's is the only show in the UK at which the dogs exhibited have to have qualified in order to be entered, thus making it the show attracting the highest-quality pedigree dogs in the country. Because of this, the show always attracts a great many visitors from abroad and has the reputation of being the premier dog show in the world.

For its centenary year in 1991 Cruft's moves yet again, this time to the National Exhibition Centre near Birmingham, in an endeavour to alleviate some of the inevitable pressures of a London show in this modern age.

## The participation of women

In 1862, three years after what was reputedly the 'first' dog show on record, two women appeared among the prize-winners at Birmingham, but it was not until 1867 that the custom of women exhibiting at shows met with approval. That was the year in which the Princess of Wales, later to become Queen Alexandra, set the fashion by exhibiting at a show held in Laycock's Cattle Sheds in Islington. Her Mastiff won second prize in its class but was officially described as 'the best ever exhibited'! In 1870 a special prize was awarded to the best dog owned by a lady, but in spite of royal example it was not until 1895 that the dog world woke up to the fact that women, who had been mere spectators for so long, intended to take a more active role. The first Ladies' Kennel Association was formed with Her Majesty Queen Victoria as Patron and a long and impressive list of Vice-Presidents, but there were many ups and downs and the association was voluntarily dissolved. In 1903 the committee was reorganised with the Countess of Aberdeen as Chairman. It was at first hoped that it might be possible to effect an amalgamation with the Kennel Club, which was then restricted to men, but alas, this was not to be. It was, however, unanimously agreed that an organisation of women dog lovers was a necessity and it was decided that they should hold a summer show at the Botanical Gardens. This turned out to be an unqualified success, assisted by the glorious weather and a record entry of 2301. The Duchess of Connaught, the President, visited the show with her family on the first day and Queen Victoria, who successfully exhibited a Borzoi and a Basset Hound, visited on the second. Here it is relevant to mention that many exhibitors did not actually show their dogs themselves but sent them along to the show with their kennel staff.

The LKA, once again active, set up new rules stating that all women were eligible for membership with the exception of undischarged bankrupts and those who were proved by the Committee to have misconducted themselves in connection with any of the objects for which the association was founded. In 1904 the show was made open to men as well as to women, exhibits hitherto having been confined to those owned by women.

In 1952 what was then known as the Cheltenham Show celebrated its twenty-first anniversary of the West of England Ladies' Kennel Society. It was decided that on this occasion all the judges should be women, and the event turned out to be a huge success with 4116 dogs making 8385 entries. The innovation was much appreciated and many well-known male judges kindly offered their services as stewards.

The Kennel Club, since its inception, had been very much a male preserve but in 1899 the Ladies' Branch was set up with restricted membership, and when in 1956 the Kennel Club moved round the corner from Piccadilly into Clarges Street much interest was aroused by the fact that the new suite of offices included a ladies' drawing room and a ladies' dining room. In 1973 the Ladies' Joint Committee was formed, initially as a watch committee – 'to watch over the rights of women'. It had been realised that a Sex Discrimination Bill would shortly come into force and it was felt that this might be sufficient to persuade the all-male General Committee to change the way the Kennel Club was run. Indeed, the Ladies' Committee felt that it was not only women who were being discriminated against but also the many thousands of men who were excluded from being members of the Kennel Club. At that time there were only about 350 members (although this number has now risen to around 750).

By 1978 the Ladies' Branch was making concerted efforts to provide for women to sit on Kennel Club committees and had been advised by solicitors that the best way to go about this would be to put up a woman for membership of the Club. It was Mrs Florence Nagle, as Chairman of the Ladies' Joint Committee, who was to be the test case. The application for membership was duly put forward and was turned down, the reason being that she was a woman. It had been known for some time that many members of the General Committee did not agree to women having equal opportunity because they did not want women in their club rooms. It was stressed that 'Mrs Nagle certainly did not wish to share the men's social activities' and that the women felt that the administrative and social sides of the Kennel Club could be separated. Mrs Nagle put her case to an industrial tribunal, but the tribunal unanimously decided that the Kennel Club was not in contravention of the Sex Discrimination Act.

The Kennel Club did, however, acknowledge that there was, as they described it, 'a wind of change blowing through the country' as far as women were concerned, and the General Committee felt that the whole position should be reviewed, dispassionately and without the coercion of a legal case. After further discussion and long involved meetings, eventually in 1979 women were at long last admitted as members of the Kennel Club, and it is interesting to note that Florence Nagle was to become one of the Club's Vice-Presidents.

## The Kennel Club today

The Kennel Club has moved its premises several times over the years but is now in Clarges Street, just off Piccadilly in London, where it employs a staff of no fewer than 120. Membership of the Kennel Club is restricted and members have a special floor for their use, but the library is open to all and houses a wealth of canine literature. The library was actually reopened in 1989 by His Royal Highness Prince Michael of Kent, and it now contains 10,000 books – reputedly the largest public collection of dog books in Europe. Also in the library are about 11,000 photographs as well as the beginnings of a video collection and a number of items of memorabilia.

The General Committee of the Kennel Club appoints a number of sub-committees to advise on different aspects of canine events, with individual sub-committees responsible for Cruft's, Breed Standards and the appointment of judges. The register of dogs recorded with the Kennel Club has been continuous since 1873 and there are now in the region of 20,000 new named dogs added to the register each year. The computerised system now holds a database of 2.6 million dogs' names and around 70,000 kennel names, known as affixes.

Another department which will be of special interest to readers of this book is that which deals with the many affiliated societies and their licensed events. There are almost 2000 such societies of varying size, holding competitions from small society events or Exemption shows, with as few as thirty dogs, to major Championship shows with up to 17,000 dogs entered. There are a number of different types of affiliated societies but Kennel Club rules governing them all follow a similar pattern. Major awards at shows are recorded in the Kennel Club Stud Book on an annual basis and each dog or bitch achieving that status is issued with a Stud Book number. The *Breed Records Supplement* is another KC publication which is issued four times each year and lists all registrations, transfers of ownership and changes of name; it also gives details of new Stud Book entries in each breed, export pedigrees and Challenge Certificate winners and those dogs to which Champion Certificates have been awarded. A recent innovation in the *Breed Record Supplement* is inclusion of the number of registered litters whelped by each bitch which has a litter recorded in that issue. Other publications are the *Year Book* which lists members, associates, affiliated societies and details of the Constitution and Regulations, and the *Kennel Gazette* which is published monthly and is of more general interest, incorporating a number of articles of a canine nature as well as many different types of announcement. Another fruit of the Kennel Club's recent labours is the *Illustrated Breed Standards* book which was published in 1989 and is designed to give information to the prospective pedigree dog owner.

Especially during the last few years the Kennel Club has been obliged to enter the political scene, having been involved in the abolition of the dog licence and other controversies such as the introduction of a mandatory registration system, overbreeding, strays and the reports of serious injuries caused by dogs. In such cases the KC has put forward a reasoned response and ministers at the Home Office and the Department of the Environment have allowed KC representatives to present their case. A 'Canine Code' has been published and a puppy pack, aimed to give information to potential dog owners, is also available in an endeavour to encourage responsible dog ownership.

# Kennel Club Junior Organisation

Set up by the Kennel Club in 1985 the KCJO, as it is most usually known, aims to encourage young people between the ages of eight and eighteen to be interested in the care and training of dogs and to enjoy all kinds of canine activities. Its purpose is primarily to promote courtesy, sportsmanship and self-discipline, and interested youngsters may become members upon payment of a small annual fee. Many events are held each year covering all aspects of the canine world – the 'KCJO Rally', a highly popular feature of the organisation, can include useful talks and practical demonstrations as well as regional visits to various interesting establishments such as Guide Dogs for the Blind, police dog training centres and veterinary surgeries. The KCJO is controlled by a Council which is appointed by the KC's General Committee and is divided into eight regions, each of which covers all the principal canine activities in its area. The KCJO can help its members to learn about stewarding, and it holds a 'Junior of the Year' competition as well as quizzes and the ever-popular KCJO Stakes classes which are scheduled at General and Group Championship shows throughout the year.

I am well aware that the novice exhibitor is by now anxious to get on and learn about how actually to go about showing, but I hope you have read this somewhat lengthy introductory chapter with patience and interest for, as I said at the outset, a knowledge of how the 'dog game' has come about will undoubtedly enhance the pleasure you will derive from it in the years to come.

# 1
# Acquiring your
# show dog

So, you have decided that you want to own a show dog and now you must begin to take steps to acquire one. You may already have decided upon the breed you would like to show, but if you have not yet done so it would be wise to give this very careful consideration from the outset.

There is absolutely no point in selecting a breed on the basis that it is numerically small, having followed the train of thought that there will be fewer dogs in each class and therefore you might stand more chance of receiving a placing. Even in numerically small breeds the competition can be very strong indeed, and it is always difficult to get past the small handful of dogs which are consistent winners because of their outstanding merits. Do not be tempted, either, to 'chop and change' breeds. Far too many exhibitors select one breed and then, finding that they do not immediately meet with the success they would like, decide to move out of that breed and concentrate on a new one with which they hope they will achieve more success. If you are highly successful with your very first show dog you will be very lucky indeed. For most exhibitors, their first dog is the one with which they get to know the ropes and it often takes many years within a breed to become established as an exhibitor and to win consistently with one's stock. In moving constantly from one breed to another you are unlikely to achieve success in any breed at all; you would be far better advised, at least for the first few years, to concentrate on showing one breed so that you get to know that breed well. Having said that, it is clear that you will need to exercise the greatest care in selecting your first show dog, for it will probably be a breed which will remain in and around your household for many years to come.

There are so many factors to consider – the size of the dog, its temperament, whether it is to be kept in the home or in an outdoor kennel, whether or not it is a breed which requires grooming or trimming (both of which can be very time-consuming). Is it a breed which needs an enormous amount of exercise, and will it get on happily with your favourite pet dog who has been with you for many years but has lived purely as a devoted companion? The list of questions you must ask yourself is endless, but if you have purchased this book you have, in all probability, already been wise enough to take these factors into consideration, so let us assume at this stage that you know which breed you want to show.

# A dog or a bitch?

Many people, when they have a clear idea in their minds about the breed they feel is the right one for them, then find themselves in the most terrible dilemma as to whether they should purchase a dog or a bitch. You may perhaps have had a certain sex before and so feel that you wish to remain faithful to that sex because you liked its temperament. But if you have not yet decided, do think carefully about this aspect because there are certain additional factors to take into consideration with a show dog. If you have a bitch there will be times at which she cannot (or should I say, preferably should not) be shown because she is in season, and often a bitch will drop coat following her season. A small breed may come into season as frequently as every six months, whereas in one of the larger breeds it may be only every eight to twelve months, depending on the breed and, indeed, on the individual bitch. There can always be exceptions, too, such as one of my own young bitches who recently managed to have her third season at only sixteen months old, thus playing havoc with her early show career. You may have heard that vets 'can give you something' to change a bitch's seasons, if one wants to delay a season for a certain reason or bring a bitch into season early. Whatever you may have heard, let me say now that my own advice is that you do not tamper with a bitch's bodily functions in this way. Many a good-tempered bitch has become nervous or even aggressive due to her owner having messed about with the pattern of her seasons, purely so that she can get to a certain show under a certain judge. The risk is simply not worth taking.

Given that seasons are undoubtedly a nuisance in that show entries may be made and have to be forfeited due to a bitch's season, it is easy to say that a dog is less difficult in this respect. However, dogs can perform differently if they have been around bitches in season or if owners have taken in-season bitches to the same show. Again speaking from personal experience, I had one super male who spent the majority of his time going round the ring like a Bloodhound (which he is not!), a habit which I simply could not break, and as a result I had to retire an otherwise good show dog. To add to the stud dog's problems, he can lose weight and condition when troubled by bitches in season. So males are not without their difficulties either.

Many people seem to feel that a bitch tends to be more loving than a dog, but I really do think that, whatever the sex, this depends largely on how the dog is brought up. If we are honest with ourselves I think we probably tend, albeit subconsciously, to treat the two sexes somewhat differently ourselves. Something which is not so relevant to the smaller breeds, but can be a very important factor when selecting one sex or the other of the larger breeds, is size and strength. Some large breeds are not easy to handle at the best of times and given that a male usually has added height, weight, power and strength, this can often sway the new owner. Another factor which I regret to say is probably true is that in many breeds it is more difficult to win with a bitch than with a dog. In many cases the quality of the bitches exhibited is higher than that of the dogs, presumably because breeders tend to keep more bitches than dogs in their kennels. It is true, too, that bitches usually get along with other members of the same sex better than dogs, especially if one or more of the dogs concerned has been used at stud, but again this very much depends upon the breed and on the individual dogs within a breed. Having said that, working on the basis that in many cases the breeder of a litter wishes to keep the best bitch (rather than the best dog), there should, in theory at least, be more good dogs available for sale to novice owners.

The decision must therefore rest with you the purchaser, and if you have made up your mind that you definitely want one sex rather than the other, don't allow yourself to be talked into the opposite sex by a breeder who will probably extol the virtues of bitches or dogs, as the case may be, simply because she has more of that sex available for sale.

# Where do I begin?

First and foremost you really should buy from a reputable breeder who shows his or her own show dogs with some success, but if the breed is new to you, you will probably not know where to start looking for the right breeders to approach. You may have seen advertisements in your local newspaper or, indeed, may know someone who has a dog of the breed you want, but your friend may not have purchased that dog from quite the sort of breeder you need to contact and so you really need to start from square one.

One way to start is to contact the Kennel Club, the address of which will be found at the end of this book, and to ask for the name and telephone numbers of the Secretaries of the specialist breed clubs for your chosen breed. Most breeds, even if they are numerically small, have at least one breed club and for the more popular breeds there are often several, usually a 'parent' club plus others which have developed on a geographical basis as the breed has grown in strength over the years. If there is more than one club for your chosen breed it would be wise to contact the Secretary of the parent club and also of the club or association which is nearest to you or covers your general area. The Kennel Club will certainly be able to provide you with this information, following which you should ideally telephone the people concerned, explaining that you are hoping to purchase a show puppy and would be grateful to have the names of some breeders who might be suitable. Of course, the final decision as to from whom you should or should not buy must be your own, but this will at least give you a starting point. When you telephone the Kennel Club you may also be told about the *Kennel Gazette*, in which some breeders advertise. Certainly this, too, will provide some of the information you require, but still, at this stage, you will have no clear indication of the integrity of the breeders who advertise, for the only stipulation made for advertisers in this medium is that they be holders of a registered affix. However, it is likely that a high proportion of them will be show people, for those who are less involved in the world of show dogs are probably not aware of this specialist magazine which is usually obtained on a subscription basis from the Kennel Club (although it can be ordered from a good newsagent and can occasionally be found on the shelves of some of the very large newsagents in major cities). You are also likely to see advertisements for puppies with 'show potential' in the weekly newspapers *Our Dogs* and *Dog World*, but again the papers make no stipulation as to the calibre of breeders who place these advertisements.

It is most important at this stage that you do not rush. Those who hurry because they cannot wait to buy their first show dog are often disappointed because the quality of the dog does not come up to expectation. Phone the breeders whose names you have acquired by all means – in doing so you will obtain some information about the prices which are being asked and you will gain some idea about those who are likely to have puppies available in the relatively near future. In addition, however, I would advise that you take yourself to a few shows to watch the

*A class of young hopefuls. Lhasa Apso puppies being shown at Bath Championship Show 1990*

breed being judged and to get into conversation with some of the exhibitors, especially those who are also breeders. It is a good idea to seek out those who are showing a home-bred dog in one of the higher classes such as Limit or Open. Depending upon the breed you have chosen you may well find that the dogs vary greatly in appearance, and by watching carefully, you should begin to develop an 'eye' for the breed and will start to get some idea of the type of breeding which appeals to you personally. A successful show dog should, of course, conform closely to the Kennel Club Breed Standard and copies of these Standards are available from the Kennel Club, although as a novice exhibitor you will probably need guidance from those more experienced than you as to how you should interpret the Standard. Reading the official Standard will, though, help you to avoid some of the fundamental mistakes – such as deciding that you would love to have a tan-coloured French Bulldog, for example, when the Breed Standard clearly states that tan is a colour which is highly undesirable. When watching a show don't, however, be too heavily swayed by the judging on the day, for different judges sometimes have very different opinions and a dog placed first by one judge may be thought of less highly by another. The exhibitors to take particular note of are those showing home-bred dogs which are 'in the cards' at the majority of Championship shows; they do not always have to win first prizes, but the very fact that their dogs are placed consistently, whoever the judge, is an indication that those exhibitors breed dogs of high quality.

For the purposes of finding out more about your chosen breed I suggest you visit a Championship show, for it is at this type of show that you will find the highest number of dogs of any one breed. The only exception to this would be to attend a breed club Open show, so when you telephone the club Secretaries ask for details of when and where their shows are held so that you may visit. You do not have to be a member of a club to go along but you may wish to consider applying to join the club, for most of them issue newsletters and sometimes booklets giving all sorts of information about the breed and keeping members advised of shows and other events which may interest them.

I mentioned getting into conversation with breeders who are exhibiting at shows. I would, however, stress that an exhibitor who is just about to take her carefully prepared dog into the ring will not appreciate a barrage of questions just at that moment. She will be wanting to concentrate 100 per cent on her dog, so watch carefully and try not to approach people when they are just about to enter a class. Also bear in mind that the dogs being shown are not necessarily being handled by their breeders for they may have been sold to other owners or may be taken into the show-ring by, for example, a professional handler. It is usually possible to buy a catalogue at a show and in this you will find all the information you want regarding the parentage of the dogs entered on the day and names and addresses of breeders and owners. To decipher which dogs have been bred by their exhibitors you will find 'Br Exh' (or something very similar) printed beside the date of birth of the dog in question; exhibitors' addresses are given at the beginning of each breed classification, or sometimes at the beginning or end of the catalogue.

When you have some idea in your mind as to which breeders' stock you rather like, you need to make specific enquiries as to whether or not they have puppies available for sale. You must make it plain that it is a show puppy you require, for no reputable breeder will wish to sell you a puppy which is well below show standard if he or she knows that you will eventually take that dog into the show-ring; that would do the breeder's reputation much harm and you, too, would be disappointed, for your dog would be unlikely to be placed very highly, if at all. But there are, I'm afraid, always some not-so-reputable, or perhaps less ex-perienced, breeders in most breeds who will cheerfully sell a pet-quality puppy as so-called 'show quality'. Quite what they are trying to achieve by doing this (other than a higher purchase price) I am never quite sure, but do do your homework and try to avoid these people for if you buy from them you will only be disappointed in the long run. To obtain a promising puppy for show you will very probably have to be prepared to wait, and you should also be prepared to travel if necessary. If the breeder you really want to buy from lives in Scotland and you happen to live in Bournemouth, you should be ready to make the journey if necessary – although I have to admit that there are advantages in having a puppy from a breeder who lives within reasonable commuting distance, for this involves less initial travelling for the puppy (though as a show dog he will have to get used to travelling) and you may be able to receive help more easily from the breeder if ever this should be needed.

# The age at which to buy

Different breeds develop at different rates so it is difficult to be specific about this aspect. However, it is certain that the older the puppy, the more sure the breeder will be as to whether the dog will or will not be suitable for the show-ring. Many experienced breeders have set times at which they like to assess the whelps. From a purely personal point of view I like to assess my own puppies at birth, ten days and three weeks, and then I keep a careful eye on them from six to eight weeks. By eight weeks I usually know which ones I have decided to sell as pets and which ones I would like to run on a little longer with a view to their ending up as show dogs. You will find that many breeders differentiate between 'pets' and 'show stock' depending on the quality of the specimen. Undoubtedly eight weeks is the very minimum age at which you should expect to buy a puppy, and if buying at this young age you are increasing the risk of something going wrong from a show point of view. The second set of teeth will not come through until the puppy is at least four months old and in some breeds there is a risk that teeth may be missing or the jaw incorrectly placed. The bones of the legs will not yet be fully developed and may not grow quite as straight as you would wish, or the hind legs may grow just slightly too much in proportion to the fore legs so that the dog's top-line is not level. Suffice it to say that the older the puppy the more sure you can be that the breeder's hunch was right and it will be suitable for showing.

Some breeders are willing to 'run on' a puppy until it is, say five or six months old, but in many cases this puppy will have to be booked in advance and you must expect to pay a much higher price than you would have paid for an eight-week-old youngster. Something to watch out for when buying a puppy of roughly this age, if it has not been booked by you in advance, is that the breeder may have run it on with the intention of showing it herself, but, as it did not quite come up to expectations, decided to sell it out. Granted, it is not easy to purchase a really top-quality show dog and most sensible breeders like to keep the very best they have bred for themselves, so if the breeder who decides to sell such a youngster is herself a highly successful exhibitor, the puppy which has been 'rejected' by her may still be very much better than a so-called 'show quality' puppy from a less experienced or less successful breeder. You will perhaps have noted that I use the term 'show quality' with some caution, for it is a term which should really not be applied to young stock. Most honest breeders will say that a puppy has show 'potential' rather than show 'quality' for it is never truly possible to state the latter until the dog is mature. Sadly, many an attractive youngster fails to make the grade in adulthood.

Another possibility is to buy a dog which has already been in the show-ring. Sometimes a breeder may campaign a youngster for a few shows and then sell it, for a substantially higher price, in view of its show wins. It may, for example, have won an award which qualifies it for the following year's Cruft's and so may be sold as 'Cruft's qualified'. Just occasionally a breeder may have a mature dog available for sale, perhaps because she has more stock than she can manage to campaign, or even because of a canine disagreement in the home, but it is rare that a breeder will part with a really high-quality adult except to another well-known exhibitor, possibly in this country but more usually abroad.

## How to select the breeder

If you have, as suggested, been to a few shows to get the feel of things you will already have some idea of the breeders who seem to be producing stock that pleases your eye. Observe the temperament of the dogs bred by these people – and you should also take more than a cursory glance at the temperament of the breeder! If the breeder seems genuinely to care for his or her dogs, treating them with kindness both in the ring and out, then the puppies raised will hopefully have been treated with love, care and attention. This is all-important, for a puppy which has had little or no affection from humans in the early weeks of its life will frequently find it much more difficult to adjust to new situations as it matures. I do not wish to imply that you should select an over-doting breeder but what you want is one who clearly cares.

You will also want to consider whether you wish to buy from one of the breed's major breeders or from someone who breeds far less often and just for a hobby. There are pros and cons for each. Clearly a breeder who produces only one or two litters a year is likely to spend more time with the puppies than the breeder who produces one or more litters a month. Having said that, the latter may perhaps have a kennel-helper who spends time with the puppies, even though the breeder's time with them is more limited. The smaller breeder is also more likely to have raised the litter in the home (thought not always) and so the puppies may be quite used to the noise of vacuum cleaners and suchlike and will therefore most probably adapt more easily to your own home environment. But those who produce fewer litters naturally produce fewer puppies and therefore fewer show puppies which, after all, is what you are looking for. In the end it is for you to assess the merits of the breeders. My advice, primarily, is to buy from someone you feel you can trust, even if it means you have to wait or travel a good distance. If the breeder shows winning stock which she has bred, that is a good sign; if the breeder in question takes into the ring only stock which has been bought in, that may be a sign that the dogs she breeds herself do not come up to the required standard for showing. Also take note of whether your selected breeder has sold successful dogs to other exhibitors – if so, this is another point in her favour.

Bear in mind, too, that it can be of infinite help for a newcomer to the show-ring to buy from someone who will also give advice – a kind of 'after-sales service' for want of a better expression. Those who are not involved with the dog may be reluctant to give constructive criticism for one reason or another, but the dog's breeder can be a great help in telling you if you are presenting the dog correctly, moving it too fast or too slowly, or perhaps entering classes which are rather too much of a challenge. A good breeder will also give you advice as to which judges you would be wise to enter under and which ones to avoid, for, if sufficiently experienced herself, she will know which judges like the kind of dogs she breeds. She may also, for example, be able to give advice such as which judges are rather too heavy-handed and should be avoided during puppyhood, not necessarily because of their lack of judgement but because of the way they go over dogs. There really is so much to consider at this very early stage, but don't worry if you have to wait a while; of course it's frustrating – you so much want to be there in the ring with your very own dog – but consider that while you are waiting you can also be learning. Keep going along to shows, watch how other people show, and pick up as many tips as you can; then when the big day finally comes you will be well prepared to make your debut.

# Breeding terms

There is always a possibility that you may be offered a bitch on 'breeding terms'. This is something favoured by some breeders and involves certain conditions of sale. These conditions are stipulated by the breeder and are many and varied, so if offered such terms do make sure that they are set down in writing and that you understand *very clearly* what the terms actually involve. In most cases the breeder will stipulate which stud dog(s) are to be used and will require at least one puppy back from the first litter produced, but I have heard of cases when the whole litter has to go back to the breeder or perhaps a specific number of puppies overall, so that if the bitch produces only one or two puppies in her first litter you are obliged to mate her again until she has produced the number agreed to in the terms set down by her vendor. Bear in mind, too, that even if the breeder requires only one puppy back, she may have stipulated that it is to be the pick of litter, so if you had hoped to breed a puppy to take into the show-ring yourself you will have to make do with what, in the bitch's breeder's opinion at least, is second best. Another stipulation often made is that the bitch must be bred from before she is a certain age, so if you have bought her with the primary aim of showing her you may find that her showing career has suddenly to be curtailed in order to honour the breeding agreement; this would be especially infuriating if you were winning well with her at the time – and remember, too, that a bitch is rarely in a condition to go straight back into the ring as soon as she has reared her litter; in a long-coated breed it can easily take a year before she once again looks the part. So I urge you to use extreme caution if offered a bitch on these terms.

On the other hand, there can sometimes be good cause to accept sensible terms. Undoubtedly it is often very difficult to buy in a really good-quality bitch, and there can be occasions when the only way to obtain one is by accepting certain terms, for the owner will simply not part with the bitch unless she has a puppy back. Indeed, many years ago I bought a bitch myself on that basis for it was the only way to get the breeding I wanted at that time. Only one puppy had to go back to the breeder, and I was careful to be sure that everything was clearly in black and white before I agreed to the transaction. As it turned out, after I had honoured this agreement and the bitch had raised her litter, I was

lucky enough for her to become a champion, so my decision to
enter into such an agreement certainly worked out well in my own
case. Sadly, however, there are many cases in which breeding
terms are either unfair or lead to unpleasantness and disagreement between the two parties concerned, so again I do urge you to
exercise caution.

# Stud terms

It is possible that you may have the chance to purchase a male
dog but that the breeder reserves the right to use him at stud,
without payment, on a specified or unspecified number of
occasions. Similarly, she may set down in the agreement that he
can be used only on certain bitches, or, for example, bitches
owned and bred by her. Such an agreement places less restriction
on your showing activities than breeding terms involving a bitch,
but do remember that a dog used at stud is frequently less clean in
the house than one which is not, and he can often become
aggressive towards other stud dogs. Add to that the fact that you
will, as a result of the agreement, probably have to play host to
in-season bitches in your home and that a dog used at stud may
become obsessed by the ladies, often making him a more difficult
dog to show. Some dogs tend not to eat when in-season bitches are
around them and so can lose that all-important 'body' which is
needed if they are to be in the peak of show condition.

As for a bitch on breeding terms, it is usual that some payment
is made for the dog purchased with stud terms, but this is usually
less than would have been asked if he had been purchased
outright. Having said that, if the quality of the dog, or indeed the
bitch, is high, the price paid at the outset may well be no mean
sum, so the whole exercise can prove to be an expensive one.

# Partnership

Another possibility you might just encounter is the offer of going
into partnership with the breeder. This most usually happens
because the breeder does not wish, for whatever reason, to
relinquish her ownership of a dog but may be content that it lives
with someone else and is perhaps shown by that same person. At
all shows entered, the names of both owners would appear in the

catalogue. Partnerships usually work best if the two (or more) people concerned actually know each other from the outset of the agreement for, just as with 'terms', all parties concerned must understand exactly what is expected of them and as partners they will need to work hand in hand over a number of years. As a newcomer to showing you could find that the dog's breeder wants to show him at whichever shows are convenient for her, relying on you merely to house, feed, groom and exhibit the dog at shows which are inconvenient for her to get to. Such a partnership is unlikely to give you much satisfaction in your new-found hobby. Another thing to be clearly defined from the outset is how the cost of veterinary bills and show fees are to be split, and who decides under which judges the dog is to be exhibited and at which shows. Agree in advance, too, how the finances would be organised if the bitch were to have a litter of puppies or if a dog were to be used at stud. Deciding these aspects when talking about a puppy of only a few weeks or months old may seem premature, but if ever you do consider entering into a partnership, everything must be clearly defined from the outset or it will simply not work well and could very easily lead to bad feeling which could have been avoided had it been approached in a professional manner from the beginning. Just remember that the dog must not be allowed to suffer as a result of any disagreements which may arise.

## Kennel Club registration

In order to show a dog he must be registered with the Kennel Club and this can be done only if he has been bred from a sire and dam who are themselves thus registered. In this way you can be sure that your own puppy's pedigree can be traced back, at least for several generations. The initial registration will have been carried out by the breeder and if you feel that there is any doubt about whether or not the puppy will be registered then steer clear, for however beautiful your new puppy may be you will not be able to show him without a certificate of Kennel Club registration, nor would you ever be able to register his or her offspring. Either at the time of purchase or shortly afterwards, the breeder should provide you with the appropriate Kennel Club documentation so that you can transfer the puppy to your ownership. As Kennel Club documents do change from time to time, it is always wise to check with the KC itself if you have any doubts at all as to whether you have the paperwork you need. You will, of course, want the puppy to be shown in your name rather than that of the breeder (unless you have reached a special agreement with the breeder for some reason), so you will need to send off your duly signed form with the appropriate fee. Remember, too, that the person from whom you bought your puppy will also have to sign the form to say that she agrees to the transfer of ownership, and do note that if he was co-bred both breeders must sign all appropriate documents. Similarly, if you decide that you wish to own your dog in partnership with another person, two signatures will always be necessary on any official documentation; under such circumstances the Kennel Club will not accept one signature and much valuable time can be lost while paperwork is sent back and forth.

# Naming

The puppy will at this stage most probably have the name given to it by the breeder, although you may have been involved in the choice of a name if your puppy was booked in advance. If you have selected your puppy's breeder with care and if that breeder is a show-goer, it is highly likely that the dog's name will begin with the breeder's affix. The affix is the name which the breeder has registered with the Kennel Club as her sort of 'trademark'; no one else may register a dog with that name. The fact that there are almost 50,000 such words already in use explains why it is that these names are sometimes rather peculiar. They cannot be words from a dictionary nor, strictly speaking, can they be place names. As an example, if the breeder's registered affix is 'Alfangum' the puppies in the litter may be Alfangum Big Sid, Alfangum Little Lilly and Alfangum Fat Fred. If, however, the puppy sold to you was not technically bred by the person from whom you bought him (this is somewhat complex, but it can happen) the puppy would most probably be called Fat Fred of Alfangum, that is to say the affix has to be used as a suffix. The only exception to this rule is if the owner of the dog bred both the sire and the dam, in which case she is at liberty to use her own affix at the front of the name.

This might all sound something of a nonsense to the uninitiated, but sooner or later you may wish to have an affix of your own so that your dogs may easily be recognised as being connected with you. In that event a Directory of Affixes can be purchased from the Kennel Club to help you to avoid those 50,000 words already selected by other breeders. If you happened to be the proud owner of Alfangum Fat Fred and wished to add your own affix which, shall we suppose, is 'Dumplety', your show boy would become Alfangum Fat Fred of Dumplety. Taking the latter case, when Alfangum is on the end of the name, you would still be obliged to add your registered affix as a suffix and add it to the end so that he may become Fat Fred of Alfangum at Dumplety. Having said that, adding a suffix constitutes a change of name and there are Kennel Club rules concerning this, one of which is that a dog's name cannot be changed after thirty days have elapsed since the dog qualified for entry into the Kennel Club's Stud Book. It is also possible that there may be an endorsement on the original Registration Certificate stating 'Name unchangeable', so it is always wise to check for endorsements and also the Kennel Club's current rules concerning this matter. On the other hand, you are not in any way obliged to add your own affix, if you have one, so Alfangum Fat Fred can remain just that and still be shown by you.

Many people new to show dogs are somewhat surprised by the length of dogs' show names. Length is not a necessity – indeed, the initial registered name must comprise more than one word but cannot be longer than twenty-four letters – but as every dog's name needs to be different from any other member of the breed registered by name within the previous ten years, the shorter the name the higher the risk of duplication. Thus it is that there is more chance of a longer name, or perhaps a rather strangely spelt name, being accepted by the Kennel Club. When applying for a dog's name you will be required to give a first and second choice when completing the necessary forms.

We shall discuss how to complete forms for show entries a little later on, but it is worth mentioning here that you, or the dog's breeder, must have applied for your dog's Kennel Club Registration Certificate prior to the first show. This certificate will include the dog's name, so if the document has not been returned to you by the time you wish to enter your dog for shows you may make the entry giving the first choice of name which has been applied for, adding after the name 'N.A.F.', indicating 'name applied for'. If the dog's registered name has been approved and you have applied for a transfer of ownership but the documentation has not been returned to you, you should add 'T.A.F.' after the dog's name, meaning 'transfer applied for'. Another possibility is that you may have applied for a change of name for your dog, in which case it is necessary to add the abbreviation 'C.N.A.F.' ('change of name applied for') if the documentation has not been returned when you are completing your entry form.

When entering into correspondence with the Kennel Club you should always enclose the appropriate fee with your documentation, for if it is not enclosed, or if the cheque (or postal order) is not of the correct value, this will cause delay. Don't forget to cross cheques 'A/C payee' and to write your name and address clearly on the back of the cheque. If you require acknowledgement of receipt you may enclose a stamped addressed postcard for the purpose.

# 2

# Training your puppy

If you are lucky your new puppy will have had a little show training with his breeder, but this will depend very much upon the breeder, the age of the puppy and whether you have made it plain that you have bought him specifically for the show-ring. With a bit of luck the breeder will already have practised a little standing and will have concentrated on this particularly with the puppies which are intended for show homes, even from the age of about six weeks. At this early stage gentle training is important because it helps the puppy to learn from a very tender age that there are times for playing and times for standing still and showing off his attributes. Indeed, it is to be hoped that most breeders will also practise with puppies destined for pet homes for, apart from helping them in the show-ring, such training is also a great help when visiting the vet's surgery for vaccinations and suchlike. A well-trained puppy is much easier for a vet to handle than one which has not learned to be controlled when necessary.

But, naturally, unless you are buying a puppy which is old enough to have already been shown by the breeder (i.e. at least six months), most of the training will be up to you. In any case, whatever the age of your new youngster, he will have moved to a completely new environment which will most probably have thrown him into confusion, so for the first few days keep training to a bare minimum and concentrate almost exclusively on getting him settled in your home. Introduce him to the various members of your immediate family, all the while making sure that no one handles him too roughly, treads on him or makes the silly joke of pulling his tail, all of which could put him off showing for life, or at least set him back a while. If you have made the decision to have a show dog it is likely that you have already had a dog as a pet, or perhaps you have one or more pet dogs living with you in the home. This gives you an undoubted advantage over someone who has never before had a dog for you will already be familiar with various aspects of the canine character (although each dog is different) and you should also know about vaccination programmes and the precautions you should take until the new youngster is fully covered. However, there will be others of you to whom dogs are completely new, or perhaps you had a dog at home with your parents but were not involved with routine vaccination programmes. In any case, there is never any harm in recapping.

## The pre-inoculation period

Depending on the age of your puppy he may or may not have begun his vaccination programme. Different vets all seem to have slightly differing theories about the safest time to give the course of injections, the differences often relating to the different vaccines used and the manufacturers' recommendations. As I write this, my own vet recommends the first injection at twelve weeks, the second at sixteen weeks and, as a safety precaution, another parvovirus injection at twenty weeks, although I do know that many vets recommend a vaccination programme which is completed a little earlier. The order in which the vaccinations are given can also vary according to the vaccine used, but they must cover distemper, infectious canine hepatitis, leptospirosis and parvovirus; many vaccines now also include protection against kennel cough. If you collect your puppy at about fourteen weeks, a wise breeder will already have begun the course of injections, in which case she must provide you with a certificate which can be passed to your own vet so that he knows exactly what vaccines have been used and when. This will be quite sufficient for him to know what is left to be done, and in case of doubt the vet can always telephone to check details with the breeder's vet, whose telephone number should be shown on the vaccination certificate.

The importance of organising your newcomer's complete vaccination programme cannot be stressed strongly enough, for if he is to be a show dog he will come into contact with a very large number of dogs at shows. Naturally one hopes that these dogs are free from disease on the show day (see Chapter 3), but one must always guard against the possibility that a dog may have been in contact with contagious disease entirely unbeknown to the dog's owner, and that that dog may be able to pass it on even though he may not have it himself. Naturally, it is just as easy for your dog to come into contact with infection when walking along the street or running in the park, so caution is the key-word at all times. Also keep in mind that if ever you need to put your dog in kennels the majority of these will not accept dogs unless the owner can provide proof that vaccinations are up to date.

The period during which the vaccination programme is incomplete is the time of highest risk so if you do have other dogs of your own you would be wise to exercise care in where you take them for walks or runs, otherwise they, too, could bring home infection to the puppy. It would be sensible, for example, to take your older dogs into the countryside for their walks rather than to a crowded park where numerous dogs have roamed. When you take your puppy to the veterinary surgeon, if he is small enough keep him on your lap or in your arms at all times for you don't know whether or not animals carrying disease have walked on the waiting-room floor. When you get into the surgery itself you should find that the vet has disinfected the table upon which he wants you to put your dog for examination; if the table shows any signs of not having been wiped down, do draw this to the vet's attention before you place your puppy on it. If you have a dog which is too large to sit on your lap in the waiting room, you should tell the receptionist that he has arrived but leave him in the car until it is your turn; if you wait in the waiting room yourself you will know when your turn comes and can carry him straight through to the consulting room. In the event of your having a dog which is genuinely too large to carry anywhere, the vet will not think you completely mad if you ask him to pop out to your car to give him his injections; this is a perfectly reasonable request if, for whatever reason, you cannot carry him, and it is much safer than allowing him to walk on the surgery floor.

While you are in the vet's waiting room, or anywhere else for that matter, don't allow people to poke unwashed fingers at your charming youngster. Of course he's delightful and it is only natural that others will want to make a fuss of him, but if you anticipate that someone is coming over to stroke him just say, 'He's not finished his course of injections yet, so I'd rather you didn't touch him please.' Most people will quite understand, and if they don't then perhaps you've taught them something! Of course you want to show off your dog, but there will be plenty of time for that later. For the time being your main aim is to keep him healthy and to help him establish his confidence in you.

# Insurance

You probably paid highly for your show dog so you may wish to consider taking out some form of pet insurance. Several companies operate such schemes and it is highly likely that your own vet will have leaflets concerning this in his waiting room. Because there are so many types of insurance and so many varying grades of cover, you should look into this fairly carefully from the outset. Suffice it to say that you will not, of course, be covered for routine injections, but should any serious problems befall your dog you could save yourself some very hefty veterinary bills. Most companies include third-party insurance which could be a great asset if your dog happened to damage someone else's property; many, however, make some restriction as to the age of the dog covered on the policy.

Some breeders actually sell the puppy with insurance for a short while; this may be included in the purchase price or may be offered as an optional extra. As already mentioned, the puppy is at its most vulnerable age pending the completion of its vaccination programme, and if the breeder has taken out an insurance, or if you are invited to do so at the time of purchase, it will usually give cover for a period of only about one month. Within that month the insurance company will usually contact you giving details of their more extensive policies so that you may take up the option of reinsuring with them if you wish to do so.

# Training in the early weeks

### Lying over

You and your dog will have much more pleasurable grooming sessions if you can learn to work together when it comes to that aspect of his care. Whether you have a long-, short- or smooth-coated breed, there will be times at which it will be an infinite advantage to have a well-trained dog which will lie over on his side. Most dogs, if trained sensibly from a fairly young age, will readily accept that when lying on their side their owners will inspect between the pads, trim the toenails and inspect ears, perhaps to pluck them or to put in ointment. If you can train your dog to lie down in this fashion you might also find it an easy position in which to put eye drops or ointment into the eyes, although personally I always do this while my dogs are in a normal sitting position. If yours is a long-coated breed there is almost no way your dog can be totally knot-free (at least not without a struggle!) unless he will lie over and, just as importantly, keep still.

It usually takes a little practice, but to get him to lie over you should stand your dog on a table (unless he really is too large in which case you will have to work on the floor), grasp the upper part of the legs which are furthest away from you and, leaning over him with your body, gently ease him down on to his side. Clearly this is a much easier task to perform with one of the smaller breeds but you will most probably find that as soon as your dog gets used to what you expect of him he will virtually roll over of his own accord, especially if you have encouraged him by talking to him and rubbing his tummy for the first minute or two so that he associates the procedure with something pleasurable. In fact, the first few times you get him to roll over, don't groom him at all, just fuss him with your hands. In those early days, if you were to do something to hurt him, such as catching the comb in a tangle, you could put him off for ever. The younger your dog is when you start practising this, the easier it will be. Begin by just brushing (the comb can come later) and go through the motions of looking inside the ears and inspecting between the toes and pads so that he gets used to you fiddling about with them. It will then come as no surprise to him when you eventually have to use the various pieces of equipment needed to keep him in trim – tweezers to pluck hair from inside the ear, scissors to trim between the pads and nail clippers to clip toenails.

I suspect that what he will be most reluctant to accept when lying down is the hairdryer, so during practice sessions switch on the hairdryer in the background, simply to get him used to the noise at this stage. When you do begin to dry him while lying down, be very careful not to pull at any knots or hurt him in any way or he will associate the dryer with pain when he is lying over. See to it also that the dryer is neither too close nor too hot. Some dogs take to this more easily than others but you will undoubtedly find that if your dog is well trained, grooming sessions are both more pleasurable and shorter!

## *Standing*

A very important aspect of training is getting your puppy used to standing still when required. In the show-ring a large breed will be required to stand only on the floor, but the Toy and smaller breeds are usually examined by the judge on the table as well as on the ground, so in the latter case you must get your show puppy used to standing still on both surfaces. A word of caution, though: when placing any dog on a table do make sure that the surface is non-slip, for if he does not feel sure of his footing, or if the table wobbles, this will certainly not help. If you have a special table set aside for the purpose (we shall come to proper show and grooming equipment later on) but it does not have a non-slip surface, you should buy a rubber car mat to place on the table, which will be perfectly adequate at this stage. Let me also stress now that, at least for practice purposes, you may need to stand, stoop or kneel, depending upon the size of your dog. Always have the dog's head facing to your right, for that is the way in which you will usually be standing in the show-ring (there are a few exceptions, such as the Peke and the Bulldog, which are shown

*From a very young age your puppy must learn to feel confident standing in a show pose. This can be practised at home*

facing the judge). In most breeds your aim will be to get the dog to stand with its feet placed naturally below the body so that the weight is evenly placed on all four feet. Again there are a few exceptions, such as the German Shepherd, which call for one of the hind legs to be extended backwards slightly, so make sure that you have taken note at the shows you have visited of the correct stance for your chosen breed.

Using a fairly firm voice, 'Stand' is the usual command, with 'No' each time the enthusiastic youngster tries to get away to do something more exciting. In many cases the breeder of the puppy may already have begun a little training in standing, for in order to assess the quality of the puppies in the litter she will have wanted them to stand calmly while she went over the various points to assess their merits. This you can practise almost as soon as you get your puppy, having first of all given him a day or two to get used to you.

By all means be firm, but under no circumstances smack the youngster for misbehaving. You should be aiming to build up his respect for you so that he looks upon you as 'top dog'; to earn his respect you can be firm but you *must* be kind. If your puppy seems particularly difficult to train you can reprimand him by staring him in the eyes and holding him firmly by the scruff of the neck, obviously keeping his back legs on the floor or, in the very small breeds, supporting the hindquarters in one of your hands. This must be done at the very moment he misbehaves so that he knows exactly what he is doing wrong. Clearly you must take care that no accident befalls you in carrying out this punishment, so don't get your face too close to his, and make sure that you have a very firm hold on the neck. It is surprising how quickly a young puppy can dart at your face (usually in play rather than as an aggressive act) when you least expect it.

## Collar and lead

Even while your puppy is not able to go out in public places, you can carry out a good deal of training in the confines of your own home. If your garden is not one which is visited by stray dogs, you can also practise outside with reasonable confidence that he is not being exposed to disease.

First of all he will need to get used to the feel of a collar around his neck, for in the show-ring he will have to be on a collar and lead, or show-lead, at all times. When a collar is first introduced

*Lead training takes a lot of patience. Here the author encourages a reluctant youngster*

this will seem very strange to him for he will have the feeling of being restricted, even when he is not. Choose a collar which is neither too tight nor too loose, for one does not want any accidents by way of your puppy getting caught up on something and consequently throwing himself into a state of panic or doing himself damage. At first you may find it easiest to use a light-weight slip-collar so that you do not have to fumble about fastening buckles while your puppy wriggles with all his might to extricate himself from your grasp! I'm afraid you cannot think of choosing a collar which will last him until he is grown up, for it would almost undoubtedly be too large, too heavy, or both. In fact this will probably be your very first lesson in coming to realise that the cost of equipment you will need to show your dog to best advantage at all times will, in the long run, amount to no mean sum.

Make sure that your puppy feels confident and is not worried by strangers or other animals around him when you first introduce the collar; he should, by now, have total confidence in you so the initial introduction is best carried out by you alone. Let him have a little smell of it first and then, holding him firmly, gently slip the collar over his head, making sure that if he does suddenly decide to panic he cannot, for example, jump off the table and hurt himself. I always like to introduce the collar while he is on the floor, however large or small the puppy. You will probably find that he doesn't even seem to know it's there at first and you may be surprised at the ease with which this new contraption has been accepted. The chances are, though, that all of a sudden he will realise that he has something strange around his neck and will paw at it in attempt to free himself; this is when you must be careful that his feet do not get stuck in it, especially if it is a slip collar which is a little more 'roomy' than an ordinary collar. Another little trick he may try is to rub his head along the ground or possibly along the bottom of your best sofa in an endeavour to slip his head out of the hole, but rarely does he succeed, although I have had one or two who have somehow managed to do it.

Practise with the collar around his neck just for a few minutes at a time at first, never allowing him to work himself up into too much of a frenzy before you take it off again. Gradually increase the amount of time he wears it, and usually within a very few days you will find that he accepts it perfectly. I would, however, stress again that in these early days you must supervise him closely when the collar is on so that he doesn't get into difficulties.

As soon as you feel that he is confident and comfortable in his collar you can introduce a lead and begin some lead training. Don't be surprised if you find that this is much more difficult than getting him used to his collar! Ideally you should use a lead which can be attached to the collar to which your puppy has already been introduced. Always choose one which fastens with a trigger mechanism rather than the sort which just slips in; the latter can easily work loose and if your puppy happens to pull in the wrong direction lead and collar can become detached so that you have one escaped puppy to retrieve. A careful choice of fastening at the end of the lead must always be a consideration throughout the dog's life, and especially so if he is exercised in busy streets where an accident could so easily happen if he were accidentally to escape. Again I would normally suggest that your choice of lead is of the relatively light-weight variety unless you have one of the large and very strong breeds which need substantial control even as youngsters. Some of the good-quality leads of man-made fabrics are both light-weight and strong, but before purchasing do check that the stitching on the lead is reliable. Like the collar, you will most probably find that you will need to purchase a heavier lead as the dog begins to reach maturity.

Many successful show-goers have their own preferences about how best to introduce the lead, and a great deal will depend upon the tractability of your puppy. However, in every case it is essential that the puppy has no distractions at all; you want him to concentrate on the job in hand and you will find lead-training much easier if you begin when you have no excited children around and when all your other pets are out of both sight and earshot. You can begin inside the house, using the largest, clearest space you can find, but it is always better, I feel, to start this part of puppy's training in the garden, using a level area of grass or paving slabs; indeed, the latter probably carry fewer interesting aromas and are therefore less likely to cause distraction. Always keep in your mind that your puppy must eventually come to associate the lead with a pleasurable experience, so make sure that you are in a happy frame of mind when you begin this training for the first time. It must be made a pleasure rather than a chore, and remember, too, that your own positive or negative vibrations will travel down the lead.

In my own case I usually begin by one of two methods. If the puppy is the sort who is somewhat bewildered by the whole affair and consequently sits stock still when you attach the lead, hold the end of the lead and move, in a backwards fashion, to the lead's length, so that you are in front of the puppy. You can then encourage him to come towards you. Give a gentle tug on the lead if necessary, but do not pull him to any extent. Make encouraging noises throughout the process and reward him with kind words and perhaps a titbit when he has reached you successfully. For the first few days' training this will be quite enough. Once again, don't practise for too long at any one time but have short sessions at various intervals throughout the day.

The other sort of puppy probably wants to scamper about madly when he finds that yet another strange contraption has been attached to the thing you call a collar, in which case he is not likely to respond readily to the above method. This sort of puppy will shoot off in a variety of directions and if you remain stationary he will get some nasty jolts each time he reaches the end of his tether. He will not yet be at the stage where you can actually lead him anywhere, so let him take you. Follow him wherever he wants to go (so you need to have chosen a suitable area which restricts him within reason), all the while holding the end of the lead but not restraining him in any way at this stage. If he suddenly realises that you are attached to the end of his lead and puts his brakes on you can then try to gain his confidence in coming towards you by using the method described above. Little and often is the motto, and within one or two days you should find that you are able to begin to guide him.

Give a very gentle tug at the lead, encouraging puppy to walk with you if possible, and keep him to your left-hand side for this is the side on which he will be expected to walk in the show-ring most of the time. But don't expect miracles at first. When he gathers that you want him to travel in your chosen direction there is every likelihood that he would prefer to go in the opposite one. He may even decide that he was born as a Jack-in-the-box and decide to leap high into the air, possibly only at occasional intervals so that you are taken completely unawares. Remember that at this stage you must still be carrying out your lead-training in the safety of your garden in an area where you are sure that he can come to no harm. It is also quite possible that a miracle appears to have happened and, at first, he walks quietly at your side like a true professional; then all of a sudden he realises what has happened and puts on his anchors. Keep his confidence at all times, encourage him gently with your voice, using his name which he probably recognises by now, and at this stage most certainly *don't shout*. It is terribly important that he associates training with a pleasurable experience, rather than the reverse. Not everyone agrees with giving titbits, but you may find that a tasty morsel is helpful for encouragement and reward at this stage, although I strongly recommend that you break the habit as soon as possible. Do, however, make sure that the chosen titbit is a suitable one; a variety of such treats are usually available from pet shops, but do avoid things like sweet biscuits of the human variety – you don't want to get him into bad habits at this age, nor do you want to rot his teeth.

By now you should be holding the lead in your left hand, with the puppy on your left, so that your right hand is free to attract him. You can make noises with your fingers or, if you like, hold a titbit in that hand, but if you are using a titbit he must be given this as a reward when he has done well; never withhold it unnecessarily or he will become confused. Don't be afraid to talk to him – a rather foolish-sounding high-pitched tone of voice often seems to go down rather well; if you can overcome your embarrassment now you will find it much easier to make your own entrance into the show-ring later on.

There are, unfortunately, some very stubborn puppies who will insist on just planting themselves firmly on their bottoms with a decided air of 'I'm not going to move, not even if a thunderbolt strikes.' These ones are awkward and training will take longer, but have patience, encourage gently rather than shout or tug too hard, and eventually the penny will drop and you will find that you have four feet trotting happily at the side of you as if there had never been any problem at all.

When your puppy's vaccination programme is complete (don't forget to wait the requisite period after the last injection if advised to by your vet) you can take him out in public, but you must still be careful that nothing will occur which may set him back a stage. By now he should be perfectly confident while walking proudly around your garden, but the big wide world outside is rather different. He is now likely to encounter sights, sounds and smells that he has never before experienced so just when you thought you'd got him going perfectly he might appear to take a slightly retrograde step. Don't be discouraged; he will soon get over it. Just remember that he must have implicit faith in you, so make sure that you instil confidence in him at all times.

Try to choose a reasonably quiet area of that big wide world to begin with. A lot will of course depend on where you live. If, for example, you live in the midst of the countryside, certainly don't begin by taking him into your local town to show him off; it is quite possible that the first bus or lorry he hears thundering towards him will turn him into a nervous, cringing wreck. Similarly, if you live in a town and decide to begin by taking him to the local park, don't begin his outside experience in the children's playground where numerous children will be shouting loudly and are likely to leap off their swings to fuss your precious show-dog. Start somewhere quiet, a country lane or a quiet corner of the park for example. Certainly it is often helpful to practise walking your youngster in noisy places eventually, but build up to this step by step rather than expect him to cope with what, to him, is a world of confusion in one fell swoop.

## Combining standing and walking

When your promising young show dog stands confidently and is conversant with the lead you can practise a short stand followed by a short walk so that he begins to get used to the sequence of events which he will encounter when he finally gets into the show-ring. If yours is a 'table dog' you can stand him on the table, then walk him a little and then get him to stand on the floor. Gradually you can begin to perfect both your own posture and that of the dog. In some of the sporting breeds the tail is held out, thereby extending the line of the back; in other breeds it is essential that the tail is carried over the back, so if it doesn't go there of its own accord, place the tail in position and keep it there by applying gentle pressure on the root of the tail with the palm of your left hand. In the Terrier breeds it may be more appropriate to stroke the tail into the desired position. Most breeds are shown to advantage with the head held reasonably high rather than in a posture which gives the impression that they are closely studying an ant burrowing in the ground; so keep your right hand under the chin to keep the head in the correct posture, but be sure not to get into the habit of letting all your fingers show on the 'show-side' so that the judge knows exactly what you're doing! In some breeds your eventual aim will be to stand away from your dog, getting him to look up at you; this is something you will have to work towards gradually for the further you are away from your exhibit the longer it takes to reach out to correct him should he decide to move at an inappropriate moment – usually just as the judge has decided to come back to give him another look over!

At a later stage you may find it helpful to look at the positioning of both you and your puppy in a full-length mirror, but it would be unwise to do this in the very early stages of training for your youngster will be distracted by the reflections he sees and it is highly likely that he will want to have a game with his new-found

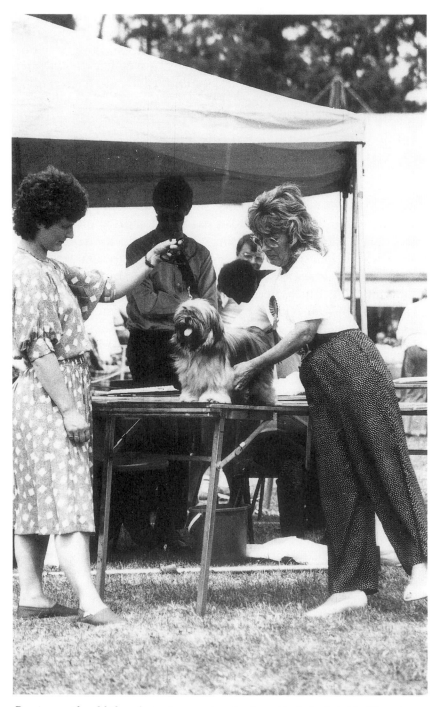

*By six months old the reluctant youngster stands on the judge's table like a true show-girl*

playmate rather than concentrate on the job in hand. It can also be useful to get a friend to watch you stand and move the puppy, giving his or her opinion on what the general appearance is from the judge's viewpoint. Naturally, it is preferable if the friend is someone with at least some knowledge of dogs so that the opinion given is one of some value to you.

## Socialisation

This brings me on to the subject of socialisation. When your puppy finally gets into the show-ring he will have to accept that the judge will want to 'go over' him in the ring. He will also come into contact with a tremendous number of strange people and strange dogs at the show, some of whom he will have to stand next to while in the ring itself. For this reason socialisation from an early age is important.

It is, however, imperative that the people and dogs with whom you allow him to come into contact, at least in the early stages of training, will not damage any confidence which you are endeavouring to build up in your puppy. Hard though it may be to accept, some people and dogs are best avoided in those early weeks. Some puppies seem to take absolutely everyone and everything in their stride, and in such a case even the roughest, toughest playmates will have no effect on them, but if, to your knowledge, a person or child is over-rough or silly with pets I feel you would be foolish to let your young puppy associate with these people in the formative weeks of his life. It can be both annoying and embarrassing to be in the very awkward position of witnessing a friend, for example, tugging at your puppy's tail and making ridiculous squeaking noises so that you want to save your puppy from the trauma and confusion but have no desire to upset the person concerned. It would be far more diplomatic to avoid your young dog coming into contact with that person to begin with, at least until you feel confident in your own mind that he can cope with the situation.

Similarly, it would be sensible to avoid aggressive and over-boisterous dogs in those early weeks. Most adult dogs have an innate awareness of a youngster's vulnerability and will take this into consideration when in play. Do always bear in mind that because the puppy's bones are not yet fully developed any injury caused may have a long-term effect on the show potential of the injured youngster. If the quickest route to the local park just happens to pass a set of gates which conceals one of those dogs which always bark loudly and viciously at passers-by (you know the type I mean), then for the sake of your show puppy you should use a different route, even if it is a little longer. I do not intend to sound over-cautious and there are, of course, those who will say, 'Well, my youngster was not affected by those situations'; all I can say is, be aware at all times that your aim is to take a confident dog into the show-ring, so you do not want him to have been unnecessarily frightened by people, noises and avoidable un-pleasant situations.

Having said that, of course your puppy will have to get used to noises and people of all kinds, but introduction to them should ideally be planned by you. People should always be encouraged to approach your dog from the front and should be told to speak a kind word to him before extending their hand. Any dog will find it much easier to accept a stranger if approached in this way rather than by a quick rub on the head (of which dogs are not very fond, by the way) followed by a verbal greeting. One of the most off-putting things for a dog is to be approached from the back, so while in the comfort of your own home, where he should feel safe and secure, get members of your close family to approach him both from the front and from the back. In the latter case, especially, they should begin by talking to him as they approach, so that he will probably turn round to look at them. Following this, the same person should again approach from the back without talking as he does so, and soon your dog will become accustomed to the fact that he may not always see or hear a person before he is touched by them.

If you know that you are going to come into contact with a noisy dog (perhaps a relative or friend has occasion to visit your home with one), try to be in physical contact with your dog personally when the other dog first barks. Your own dog should then be somewhat reassured by your presence and will not be afraid. It is not, however, a good idea to over-protect your dog for any anxiety or fear felt by you will also be communicated to your four-legged friend.

But the sounds of dogs and people are not the only noises his sensitive ears will have to suffer. Only too often at a show you have just positioned your dog perfectly for the judge when a plane flies overhead or a vociferous Show Secretary makes an announcement over the tannoy and, if you are unfortunate, the loudspeaker is located right above your ring. There is, of course, absolutely nothing you can do about this but it will certainly be to your dog's advantage if he is not put off by the sound and continues to show like a Trojan, even though you and the judge may not be able to hear yourselves speak. Other unfortunate happenings which seem to occur all too regularly include a strong wind which blows down the award board, making an almighty clatter or a loud thud as one of the bench seats collapses by the ring, throwing its solitary occupant to the floor. I do not suggest that you set up a tannoy system at home with which to practise, nor that you invest in collapsible furniture with which to experiment, but I do think you would be well advised to create a little noise from time to time. Turn the radio up more than usually high occasionally; it is always a good idea to let dogs get used to the various voices they can hear on the radio so select a channel which has plenty of chat programmes so that they will hear a wide variety of voices. (Digressing for a moment, if you have a dog which is distressed when you leave it alone in the house, you may well find that leaving a radio on will help to solve the problem.) Another useful noise is the clatter of saucepans, the volume of which you can regulate at will, depending upon the size of the pans. Never make an attempt to frighten your youngster deliberately but try to involve him in as much household activity as possible so that even the most unlikely situation he meets in the show-ring will not put him off.

We talked earlier about where you can take your puppy to practise his lead-training, and I would stress that you should not rush into taking him to busy areas too soon. But when you feel he is sufficiently confident you can start to introduce him to new areas so that he becomes familiar with different ground surfaces, smells and general sounds. A most useful exercise which I have used successfully in the past is to take a dog, after shopping hours, into an enclosed shopping mall. The first time I did this I was interested to see that my puppy was at first reluctant to go from one type of floor tile to another, differently coloured one; when he came to a narrow metal grid he stopped dead and would not tread over it at any price. However, within half an hour or so he was merrily trotting over any new texture we could find without even stopping to think. Another good thing about a shopping mall is that the acoustics are very different from the open air and the sound of your feet can echo loudly. Remember that when you take your dog to a show it will not always be outdoors; winter shows especially are held in indoor venues, often with uncomfortably high ceilings which must seem very strange when encountered for the first time. In inclement summer weather shows can also be moved inside at the venue; 'inside' may be a hall of some type, but it could equally well be a cattle shed or a marquee which makes a strange flapping noise as it is battered by wind and rain. No, you don't have to erect a marquee in your garden; all I am saying is that when you feel your puppy is confident on the lead, gradually introduce him to different surroundings so that nothing will come as a surprise. Sadly my own nearest shopping mall is now many miles away, and many of them do not allow dogs inside anyway, even after hours – but perhaps you can find a suitable compromise. Do remember that wherever you take your dog in public you must be prepared to clean up after him if he has an accident. Proper dog scoops are available but a polythene bag will do just as well; you can scoop up, tie the bag and suitably dispose of the excreta without offending anyone, except perhaps those onlookers who can't quite believe their eyes and who have absolutely no comprehension of what responsible dog ownership actually involves. We canine enthusiasts and our animals suffer quite enough from the anti-dog lobby. Don't, under any circumstances, give them cause to complain further.

# 3

# Your show dog comes out

Until now your main aim has been to build up your puppy's confidence in you and to help him become accustomed to various environments. With any luck he will, by now, walk with relative ease on the lead, stand in something resembling a showmanlike posture, and lie on his side for the purposes of grooming or inspection of such parts of his anatomy as toenails and pads. Now is the time to decide what step to take next.

## Ringcraft classes

Let me begin by saying that there are many highly successful exhibitors who never take their dogs to ringcraft classes, but if you are a novice exhibitor this can be an ideal training ground for both you and your dog. A ringcraft class is usually run on a non-profit-making basis and is for the specific purpose of training show dogs for the show-ring. It is not to be confused with an obedience class which helps you to teach your dog to sit, for example, on command. When you take your dog to a show and have finished moving him for the judge, you will want him to stand, not sit, so be careful not to get confused from the outset with these two types of training class. Some show dogs also go to obedience classes and, indeed, some non-show dogs go along to ringcraft for the fun of it, but in the early stages of training I would strongly recommend that you attend ringcraft only, otherwise both you and your dog run the risk of becoming totally confused.

I recommend such classes with caution, for there are the good and the not so good. Bearing in mind that the people who organise them do so on a purely voluntary basis, the 'trainers' can be of varying talents themselves, and unfortunately there are cases when people with very limited personal experience are called in to help. So it is that you must select your training class with the greatest care.

If you are in one of the numerically strong breeds you may be lucky enough to find that the regional club for your breed holds classes on a regular or semi-regular basis. Such classes should be ideal, for here you will undoubtedly come into contact with people within the breed who are much more experienced than you and from whom you can learn a great deal about your chosen breed. At the other extreme, if yours is a breed for which there are only one or two clubs nationally it is highly unlikely that they will offer such classes because the club's membership will be too widespread. Indeed, if you do not live in or near a town or city you may find that your nearest class is many miles away, the reason being that such classes usually take place in a hired hall and therefore organisers have to be sure that a good few people will attend in order to cover the costs.

The Kennel Club can give details of those training clubs registered with them, but not all such classes are organised by registered clubs. The best way of finding out which is likely to be the most suitable class for you is to ask someone who lives locally and is an enthusiastic and preferably successful exhibitor in a breed similar to your own. By similar, I mean that if you have a table dog you should seek the advice of someone who also has one of the smaller breeds, whereas if yours is a large Gundog you would be better advised to talk to someone who is also in one of the larger gun breeds, for two such extremes will need to be handled differently. If you are lucky enough to have bought your dog from a breeder/exhibitor who lives reasonably locally, then she is the obvious person to ask.

When you have located the class which you believe to be the most suitable (not always the most convenient one, I'm afraid) you can usually go along on the first night with no obligation to join the club. The system is usually that one pays a token membership fee as well as a small sum each time one visits. You may decide not to take your dog along with you on that first evening, or, if it is a cool evening, it could be sensible to leave him in the car until you are sure it is the sort of place which will not be too much of a shock to his system. If, for example, you have a tiny Toy and the only dogs there are big, heavy, fast movers, then you may be wise to look elsewhere. Most classes have a fairly good selection of breeds but others get a reputation for training one type of dog especially well and, as a result, get a predominance of that breed. Fine if that breed happens to be your own, but not so good otherwise. Just remember that you don't want to put him off showing at this stage. You don't need to be over-protective, for he must come into contact with all sorts of dogs sooner or later, but do use your own judgement and if there is a selection of classes available make sure that you choose the very best.

It is always a good idea to start by watching with your dog, at least for the first part of your initial visit. This gives you the opportunity to assess the merits of the trainers while your dog gets used to the sounds around him; if you can see, for example, that one of the trainers is going over the dogs too roughly or does not know how to open a dog's mouth to inspect the teeth (sadly some don't), then wait until another trainer takes the centre of the floor, even if that means waiting until another week. At most clubs the trainers work on some sort of a rota system so that the dogs get used to different 'judges'. They may change over at the coffee break, or if the hall is large enough there may be two trainers working at the same time; others invite a different trainer each week. Keep in your mind at all times that you are there to train your dog to show his very best when he finally gets into the real show-ring, and that your dog's well-being is of paramount importance.

Of course, each ringcraft class is run in its own way, according to the organisers, but most give you plenty of opportunity to stand your dog in line with other dogs, to move them around the 'ring' together if the venue is large enough, and to stand and move your dog just as you would be expected to in the real show-ring. In some cases there may even be mock placings at the end of each evening, for in this way the exhibitors have practice in being 'pulled out' and the dogs get used to the sound of clapping from the ringsiders, both of which can be off-putting at first. Many clubs arrange matches against other clubs on an occasional basis, which adds a little variety to the weekly routine and enables the dogs to be in a virtual show situation. A Kennel Club Licence will have been applied for by the host club and the match has to take the form of one dog against one, so that the eventual winner has won by process of elimination. Usually a local judge is invited to officiate and all exhibitors must be members of one of the participating clubs, added to which each dog can be exhibited only by his owner, as registered with the Kennel Club. A club can hold up to twelve matches each year, so some clubs arrange such an event on a monthly basis. Certainly attendance at ringcraft classes and matches has the advantage of bringing you into contact with other people who live locally and who enjoy showing their dogs, and some consider them quite a social occasion. You can learn a lot from many of these people, but bear in mind that most of them are unlikely to be experts in your chosen breed, so don't take everything that is said as the gospel truth. Many seasoned exhibitors find it helpful to take their young show stock along to classes for a few weeks until they are old enough to gain experience at actual shows. Equally, if one has a difficult dog to show it can be helpful to take him along to ringcraft to get in a little extra practice between shows.

# Condition

## *Coat*

If you want to give your dog every opportunity of being placed as highly as possible at shows you must be sure that he is kept in tip-top condition. The specific coat preparation you need will be relevant to your own special breed so you must seek breed specialist advice on how to look after your dog's coat. There is not space here to give details of show preparations for each breed of dog, but before you selected your breed you should have obtained, or at least had access to, books especially about the breed, and most of these incorporate at least some information concerning coat care. So if you haven't already armed yourself with books about the breed, do so now. It is a good idea to go to a large library and look through the books on their shelves so that you get some idea of which ones give the greatest amount of useful information; you can then usually buy the books of your choice from any good bookseller, although you may have to wait a few weeks for your order if it is not a stock item. However, if you have already made your way to Championship shows you will have discovered that some of the trade stands have excellent book sections where all manner of canine material is available, and here you will almost certainly find the book of your choice.

If you are to show a long-coated breed, it will be imperative that you look after the coat with care between shows, for it is the long coats which pick up the greatest amount of debris while in the garden or on walks. Always make sure that whenever your dog comes into the house or is put into his kennel every little bit of twig is removed, for if it is allowed to remain in the coat it will become entangled and a knot will have formed before you know it. If the coat gets wet it should be dried off as soon as possible but, in a long-coated breed, always pat the coat dry rather than rub because rubbing a coat dry will cause those unwanted tangles. If you really want to promote length of coat and if yours is one of the long-coated breeds, the furnishings of which actually reach the ground, you will also have to give great consideration to the type of surfaces you allow him to run on or you will find yourself fighting a losing battle. In some breeds, such as the Yorkshire Terrier, it is the practice to wrap the coat so that the ends do not break, but this is something which, as you will appreciate, needs expert guidance; so seek the advice of your dog's breeder or the specialists within the breed.

Other breeds which need a good deal of time spent in coat care are those which are trimmed or stripped for show. If you have one of these breeds you really must learn properly how to care for the coat for the appearance of even the best dog can be ruined by incorrect preparation. It takes time and practice to become proficient in both trimming and stripping, so start watching other exhibitors as soon as you possibly can and seek guidance and tuition well before your puppy reaches maturity.

The coats of the shorter- and smooth-coated breeds also need some attention, so see that they, too, are kept in good order between shows. If, for example, your dog's supposedly shiny coat looks a little on the dull side, a drop of oil in the diet will be found to help.

How frequently you should bath you dog will again depend upon the breed. In some breeds it is considered taboo to bath the dog at all, but remember that no judge wants to put his hands on a dirty, smelly dog, so if yours is one of the breeds for which bathing is not recommended (this recommendation usually being made so as not to soften the coat) you will have to find a way of keeping the coat clean and in good order throughout the dog's life, for neither do you want a dirty smelly dog around your house!

At the other extreme there are some breeds that the majority of exhibitors bath on a weekly basis, or at least before every show. This is, of course, time-consuming and you should have considered this aspect before you chose your breed. If yours is one of these breeds, and especially if your dog's coat is long, you will very probably need to invest in a professional canine hairdryer which will cut down the drying time substantially and will allow you to get a better finish on the coat, because it is free-standing so that both your hands are available for grooming. Such dryers are by no means cheap but those of the best quality can give you many years' service. You can see a variety of such dryers on display at most general Championship shows and, just a little word of warning, do ask if you need to keep in stock any spare parts because if, for example, a washer goes and you can't get one to fit at your local shops, you might find yourself in an awkward predicament the night before a show. Most companies which sell canine hairdryers do, however, operate a postal service which can often be a godsend.

If you do need to bath your dog – and let's face it, those show dogs which are not bathed are the exception rather than the rule –take care also in the selection of shampoo. Use one designed for canines rather than humans and don't choose one which is designed to soften the coat unless you actually want a soft coat. You will find a very wide variety of shampoos and conditioners on sale at shows, so do read the bottles carefully before you make your purchase.

But coat preparation and presentation are by no means the only factors involved in getting your dog in condition for the show-ring.

### General condition

Different breeds mature at different rates, and if your breed is new to you, you must seek advice from the breeder as to whether or not you should exercise your dog greatly in the early months of its life. For many of the large and giant breeds it is considered wise to restrict exercise at first, for the bones develop at such a fast rate and the legs and feet have to support great body weight. It may be suggested, for example, that your puppy exercises freely only in a limited area until he is five or six months old, following which you take him for walks of up to a mile for a month or so, building up slowly to two miles and so on until, by the age of a year, your dog should be walking four miles a day on a lead plus having the opportunity to exercise freely, for he will naturally take rest when exhausted. There are so many different stipulations for the various breeds, but the above will give you some idea of what you can expect if you have one of the larger breeds. Also take advice as to which food supplements you should give while your dog's bones are still growing; often a calcium supplement is a useful addition to the diet.

With the smaller breeds the major stipulation made is that a youngster should not jump on and off furniture, for in doing so he will run the risk of forcing out his elbows due to the front legs taking too much pressure as the dog lands. Stairs, too, should be treated with caution.

Especially for those adult dogs which are kept in a home and therefore spend a large proportion of their time on carpeted floors, some road work will be necessary. Moving at a steady pace on hard surfaces will help to tone up the pasterns and if the dog also gets free exercise on grass his feet will have the opportunity to move in various different ways, thus allowing them to develop to the full. Free exercise on grass will also give tone to the muscles and will allow limbs to be fully extended.

## Feeding

Without correct feeding no dog will reach the peak of condition; feed too much or too little and your dog will not look his best. Some dogs are prone to carrying too much weight, in which case the quantity of food will have to be reduced or it may be necessary to change the type of food given. On the other hand, some dogs seem always to look a little underweight despite the fact that they eat large quantities of food. I always find that tripe is good for putting on weight but if you feed raw tripe don't forget to keep to a regular worming programme, and it is, of course, always safer to feed your dog tripe which comes from animals which have been slaughtered for human consumption, rather than from a knacker's yard.

Another thing to watch is the protein content given in food. All dried and tinned foods will give the exact protein content on the outside of the sack or on the tin. If you buy your dried food in small quantities you may find that it is packed in polythene bags by the retailer, in which case make sure you check the sack in the shop before you make your purchase. As a general guide a young puppy will require a high protein content, but this will need to be reduced by the time he reaches maturity. A dog which is hyperactive should have his protein content reduced, but on the other hand, a dog which is given a great deal of exercise, possibly because he is used in sport or in work, needs a higher protein intake because of the energy he uses.

A healthy, correctly fed dog is likely to have a good coat condition and will have that certain sparkle in his eyes which gives both you and the judge the signal that all is well.

# Time to show

In the UK a puppy has to be a minimum of six months old before he can be exhibited at a show, but you will be surprised how quickly the time approaches, particularly when you bear in mind that entries for a show have to be made sometimes several weeks in advance. Let us begin by looking at the various types of show at which you can exhibit your dog.

The shows you attend must be held under Kennel Club Licence and the Licence must be on display at the show. As all major shows are licensed in this way this need not concern you greatly unless you attend Exemption shows, at which entries are made on the day. There is always the chance, if you live in the depths of the countryside as I do, that local farmers will organise a dog section in their village fete and simply don't realise that a Kennel Club Licence is a must. So do check, or you could end up in trouble with the KC if you were to exhibit or officiate at the show.

## Exemption Shows

These are undoubtedly the most informal type of show and any funds raised usually go to some worthy cause. There are usually not more than four classes for pedigree dogs and these must be Any Variety classes, meaning that they are open to dogs of different breeds. A fifth pedigree class can be scheduled if it is exclusively for dogs exhibited by people under the age of eighteen; the dogs must be owned either by the exhibitors or by their parents. Indeed, the show itself is open also to cross-breeds and mongrels which can join in the novelty classes, such as 'Dog with the waggiest tail', etc. Such shows can be fun; the atmosphere is relaxed, the entry fees are cheap and because entries are taken at the show you can decide on the day whether or not you and your dog feel like an outing to a show. Exemption shows can be used as a training ground for youngsters, but keep in mind at all times that not all the dogs which attend are show dogs, and because of this you may come across dogs of varying temperament and, more importantly, their owners may not be proficient in keeping control of them. Judges at such shows are frequently experienced judges, but not always, so don't be too disappointed if you don't win. It will probably come as a relief to know that no dog holding an award which counts towards the title of Champion is allowed to enter. Treat an Exemption show more as a fun day than as a serious event and you and your dog will probably thoroughly enjoy your day out.

Details of Exemption shows are often found in local newspapers, libraries and veterinary surgeries as well as in the canine press. Entry for the show cannot be made in advance but has to be done at the show itself. It is also not usually necessary to enter all your classes at the beginning of the show. You may prefer to see how quickly the judging is going or how easily your dog is settling down, and in most cases you may therefore make an entry in a subsequent class when the day's judging is already in progress.

## Primary Shows

This is a rare type of show indeed, for in all my years of dog showing I have never come across one, so I don't think we need to delve too deeply into these as you, like me, will probably never hear of one. Briefly, you have to become a member of the society if you are to make an entry, and the show can offer a maximum of eight classes which must be held after 5 p.m., except at weekends and on public holidays when they may begin at 2 p.m. The exhibits are restricted to those who have never won a Challenge or Reserve Challenge Certificate, nor a first prize at a show unless it has been won in one of the puppy classes. Perhaps this is why such shows presently seem to be so unpopular!

## Sanction Shows

Again, at a Sanction show one has to be a member of the organising society (membership can usually be applied for at the time of entering the show) and there are restrictions on the number and type of classes which may be scheduled. No class at a Sanction show may be higher than Post Graduate.

## Limited Shows

Such shows are also limited to members, and again it is generally possible to join the society at the same time that you make the show entry. At Limited shows dogs which have won a Challenge Certificate or any award which counts towards the title of Champion are not allowed to compete, but this type of show generally has a greater selection of classes on offer than the preceding types.

## Open Shows

There are no restrictions in force at these shows. This means that one does not have to be a member to enter the show, although sometimes the society stipulates that trophies on offer may be held only by members. Dogs which are champions can be entered for the show, but in most breeds it is somewhat frowned upon by other exhibitors if owners of Champions constantly take them round to all the local shows, although technically there is nothing to prevent them from doing so. At an Open show there is often a very good selection of classes on offer, many of which are for specific breeds only while others are for variety competition (i.e. open to more than one breed). Some Open shows have benching regulations but most do not, and entry fees are usually quite reasonable.

*At an unbenched Open show the atmosphere is informal and relaxed. Provided there is sufficient space between rings, dogs can enjoy their owners' company throughout the show*

## Championship Shows

A Championship show is one at which Kennel Club Challenge
Certificates are on offer. Again, membership of the society is not
necessary. Some Championship show societies allow people to
join as associate members for a small fee. To become a Champion
a dog has to obtain three Challenge Certificates, commonly
known as 'CCs', under three different judges. At least one of those
CCs must be awarded after the dog has reached the age of twelve
months. General Championship shows are very large indeed;
they are usually spread over about a three-day period and the
dogs are all benched, although some breed clubs manage to
obtain exemption from benching for their breed club Championship shows.

## Finding out about shows

Throughout your time as an exhibitor you will need to purchase,
or at least have access to, either or both of the canine weekly
newspapers, *Our Dogs* and *Dog World*. These can be purchased
over the counter from some of the very large newsagents but you
would be better advised to order them from your local one, as few
shops carry many spare copies. Dog shows are listed in the section
at the back of each of these newspapers but specialist breed shows
are sometimes included in the 'breed notes' columns, so don't
forget to look there too. Most show societies place the same
advertisement in both papers so even if you buy only one you are
not likely to miss details of shows.

Advertisements will give the name of the show society and the
location of the show; always check the latter when you are
planning your journey time for a show can frequently take place
several miles away from the named town of the show society, the
ample facilities of the Three Counties Show Ground at Malvern
being an example of a venue which hosts several shows run by
societies based many miles apart. It is the availability and
suitability of the venue which determines the actual location of
the showground.

Also in the advertisements you will usually find the breeds
which are to be judged, together with the relevant judges' names
beside them (these can be before or after the breed name, so read
from the beginning of the list so as not to be mistaken). Some of
the abbreviations used can be a little confusing at first, so the

following list of the most common abbreviations may be of
assistance.

| | |
|---|---|
| AV | Any Variety |
| NSC | Not Separately Classified |
| AVNSC | Any Variety Not Separately Classified |
| CKCS | Cavalier King Charles Spaniels |
| GSD | German Shepherd Dogs |
| OES | Old English Sheepdogs |
| SBT | Staffordshire Bull Terriers |
| WHWT | West Highland White Terriers |
| L/C | Long Coated |

The following abbreviations are used for the awards made
following competition between some or all of the unbeaten dogs.

| | |
|---|---|
| BIS | Best In Show |
| RBIS | Reserve Best In Show |
| BOB | Best Of Breed |
| RBOB | Reserve Best Of Breed |
| BOS | Best Opposite Sex |
| BP | Best Puppy |
| BPIS | Best Puppy In Show |

Often a number will appear in brackets by the breed name and
this indicates the number of classes scheduled under that
heading. By the side of the name of the judge it is common also to
find the judge's affix, which will probably help you to distinguish
exactly which 'Mr Smith' is judging your breed. Occasionally,
presumably because the judge concerned does not have an affix,
instead you will find his home county beside his name, for
example 'Mr Smith (Bucks)'.

Don't be confused by the fact that two dates are given in the
advertisement. One is the date of the show, while the other is the
closing date for entries. This indicates not the date on which the
entries have to be received by the Show Secretary but the latest
date on which they can be posted using first-class mail. It is
relevant here to mention that all Show Secretaries very much
appreciate entries being posted a few days before the scheduled
closing date if at all possible. There are always a few exhibitors
who manage just to miss the last post, and the strange thing is
that they are frequently the same exhibitors. Strictly speaking,
the Show Secretaries are well within their rights to refuse any
entries not showing a postmark with the correct date, so please

*don't post late.* As much as we appreciate our postal services, there can always be unusual delays, especially around Christmas time, so do try to help Show Secretaries as much as you can by complying with the rules. When they receive the entries their work is nowhere near over; everything has to be checked and sorted out for the catalogue printers, and nothing can be allowed to hold up the show.

During your first year as an exhibitor you will have a great deal of writing or telephoning to do. To obtain a schedule you should ideally write to the Secretary, enclosing a stamped addressed envelope, but if time does not permit you may telephone. The relevant address and telephone number can be found in the advertisement. However, once you have entered a show you will usually find that schedules of subsequent shows organised by that society are mailed to you automatically, although if you then fail to enter one of their shows your name will generally be removed from the mailing list and you will have to re-apply. If you are a member of a breed club you will usually find that schedules are automatically sent to you for each show organised by that club.

You will notice that the closing date for entries is some weeks before the show. Entries for General Championship shows frequently close about a couple of months prior to the show date; for Open shows the close is four or five weeks beforehand, and for Limited and Sanction shows roughly three or four weeks. As mentioned earlier, if you intend to exhibit your puppy from the age of six months you will need to look out for shows to enter from the time he is about four months old.

## How to enter

When the show schedule arrives it will have with it an entry form which you will need to complete carefully and return to the address given on the form by the due date. Let us deal first of all with the schedule, for this is the section which gives you all the information you will need about the show. The layout can vary slightly but usually on the front cover, along with details of the venue and names of some of the organisers, you will find the time at which the show opens and the time at which judging commences; this is not necessarily the time at which you will be in the ring with your exhibit – it is the time when judging begins for those breeds which are scheduled first in the ring. Some show societies (but by no means all) also give an indication of the time at which each individual breed is likely to be judged. They are, however, at liberty to change this if necessary, so the onus is on you to get to the show in good time. Upon arrival at a show it is always wise to listen for announcements for it is sometimes necessary for changes to be made to the order of judging or to ring numbers; it is your responsibility to be sure that your dog is presented for judging at the correct time and in the correct ring.

Inside the schedule you will find the various rules as stipulated by the Kennel Club together with a list of the classes scheduled for each breed. These will be given names such as Puppy, Novice, Post Graduate and Open. Elsewhere in the schedule, for easy reference, you will find the definitions for each type of class at that show. We shall cover record-keeping later on, but do take care that you keep track of your dog's wins, for a dog which has, for example, won three first prizes in Novice classes at Open shows is no longer eligible to enter such a class again. The following is a full list of definitions, reproduced by kind permission of the Kennel Club.

In the following definitions:

* applies to Championship and Open Shows only
** applies to Limited, Sanction and Primary Shows only.

Where there is no qualification, the definition applies to all types of shows.

In estimating the number of awards won, all wins up to and including the seventh day before the date of closing of entries shall be counted when entering for any class.

Wins in Variety Classes do not count for entry in Breed Classes, but when entering for Variety Classes, wins in both Breed and Variety Classes must be counted. A First Prize does not include a Special Prize of whatever value.

| | |
|---|---|
| MINOR PUPPY | For dogs of six and not exceeding nine calendar months of age on the first day of the Show. |
| PUPPY | For dogs of six and not exceeding twelve calendar months of age on the first day of the Show. |
| JUNIOR | For dogs of six and not exceeding eighteen calendar months of age on the first day of the Show. |

BEGINNERS

\* For owner, handler or exhibit not having won a First Prize at a Championship or Open Show

\*\* For owner, handler or exhibit not having won a First Prize at any Show.

MAIDEN

\* For dogs which have not won a Challenge Certificate or a First Prize at an Open and Championship Show (Minor Puppy, Special Minor Puppy, Puppy and Special Puppy classes excepted, whether restricted or not).

\*\* For dogs which have not won a First Prize at any Show (Minor Puppy, Special Minor Puppy, Puppy and Special Puppy classes excepted, whether restricted or not).

NOVICE

\* For dogs which have not won a Challenge Certificate or three or more First Prizes at Open and Championship Shows (Minor Puppy, Special Minor Puppy, Puppy and Special Puppy classes excepted, whether restricted or not).

\*\* For dogs which have not won three or more First Prizes at any Show (Minor Puppy, Special Minor Puppy, Puppy and Special Puppy classes excepted, whether restricted or not).

TYRO

\* For dogs which have not won a Challenge Certificate or five or more First Prizes at Open and Championship Shows (Minor Puppy, Special Minor Puppy, Puppy and Special Puppy classes excepted, whether restricted or not).

\*\* For dogs which have not won five or more First Prizes at any Show (Minor Puppy, Special Minor Puppy, Puppy and Special Puppy classes excepted, whether restricted or not).

DEBUTANT

\* For dogs which have not won a Challenge Certificate or a First Prize at a Championship Show (Minor Puppy, Special Minor Puppy, Puppy and Special

Puppy classes excepted, whether restricted or not).

** For dogs which have not won a First Prize at an Open or Championship Show (Minor Puppy, Special Minor Puppy, Puppy and Special Puppy classes excepted, whether restricted or not).

UNDERGRADUATE * For dogs which have not won a Challenge Certificate or three or more First Prizes at Championship Shows (Minor Puppy, Special Minor Puppy, Puppy and Special Puppy classes excepted, whether restricted or not).

** For dogs which have not won three or more First Prizes at Open or Championship Shows (Minor Puppy, Special Minor Puppy, Puppy and Special Puppy classes excepted, whether restricted or not).

GRADUATE * For dogs which have not won a Challenge Certificate or four or more First Prizes at Championship Shows in Graduate, Post Graduate, Minor Limit, Mid Limit, Limit and Open classes, whether restricted or not.

** For dogs which have not won four or more First Prizes at Open or Championship Shows in Graduate, Post Graduate, Minor Limit, Mid Limit, Limit and Open classes, whether restricted or not.

POST GRADUATE * For dogs which have not won a Challenge Certificate or five or more First Prizes at Championship Shows in Post Graduate, Minor Limit, Mid Limit, Limit and Open classes, whether restricted or not.

** For dogs which have not won five or more First Prizes at Championship and Open Shows in Post Graduate, Minor Limit, Mid Limit, Limit and Open classes, whether restricted or not.

MINOR LIMIT * For dogs which have not won two Challenge Certificates or three or more

First Prizes in all at Championship Shows in Minor Limit, Mid Limit, Limit and Open Classes, confined to the breed, whether restricted or not at Shows where Challenge Certificates were offered for the breed.

** For dogs which have not won three or more First Prizes in all at Open and Championship Shows in Minor Limit, Mid Limit, Limit and Open classes, confined to the breed, whether restricted or not.

MID LIMIT
* For dogs which have not won three Challenge Certificates or five or more First Prizes in all at Championship Shows in Mid Limit, Limit and Open classes, confined to the breed, whether restricted or not at Shows where Challenge Certificates were offered for the breed.

** For dogs which have not won five or more First Prizes in all at Open and Championship Shows in Mid Limit, Limit and Open classes, confined to the breed, whether restricted or not.

LIMIT
* For dogs which have not won three Challenge Certificates under three different judges or seven or more First Prizes in all at Championship Shows in Limit and Open classes, confined to the breed, whether restricted or not at Shows where Challenge Certificates were offered for the breed.

** For dogs which have not won seven or more First Prizes in all at Open and Championship Shows in Limit and Open classes, confined to the breed, whether restricted or not.

OPEN
For all dogs of the breeds for which the class is provided and eligible for entry at the Show.

VETERAN
For dogs of not less than seven years of age on the day of the Show.

| CHAMPION | For dogs which have been confirmed a Champion, Show Champion or Field Trial Champion. |
| RARE BREEDS | Confined to those breeds not granted Challenge Certificates in the current year, with the exception of those breeds whose registration is confined to the Imported Register. |
| FIELD TRIAL | For dogs which have won prizes, Diplomas of Merit or Certificates of Merit in actual competition at a Field Trial held under Kennel Club or Irish Kennel Club Field Trial Regulations. |
| WORKING TRIAL | For dogs which have won prizes in competition at a Bloodhound Working Trial and Kennel Club licensed Working Trials, held under Kennel Club Regulations. |
| STUD DOG | For stud dogs and at least two progeny of which only the progeny must be entered and exhibited in a breed class at the Show. |
| BROOD BITCH | For brood bitches and at least two progeny of which only the progeny must be entered and exhibited in a breed class at the Show. |
| PROGENY | For a dog or bitch, accompanied by at least three of its registered progeny. The dog or bitch not necessarily entered in another class however, all progeny having been entered and exhibited in another class. The dog or bitch and the progeny need not be registered in the same ownership. |
| BRACE | For two exhibits (either sex or mixed) of one breed belonging to the same exhibitor, each exhibit having been entered in some class other than Brace or Team. |
| TEAM | For three or more exhibits (either sex or mixed) of one breed belonging to the same exhibitor, each exhibit having been entered in some class other than Brace or Team. |
| BREEDERS | For dogs bred by the exhibitor. |

| IMPORTED REGISTER | For breeds whose registration is confined to the Imported Register, and which consequently may only be entered in this class. |
| ANY VARIETY NOT SEPARATELY CLASSIFIED | For breeds of dog for which no separate breed classes are scheduled. |
| NOT FOR COMPETITION | Societies may, at their discretion, accept Not for Competition entries. Societies may accept such entries from breeds of dog not included within the title of the Society, and at Shows held over more than one day, such entries may be accepted on any day from any breed. |

## Which classes to enter

As you will have noticed in the above listing, some of the classes are defined by age of the exhibit and others by previous wins. Technically speaking, a puppy which has never won a first prize in a class other than those scheduled for puppies is eligible to enter any other class scheduled for the breed (unless, perhaps, it is a 'Special' class) and it is this which causes many novice exhibitors to enter inappropriate classes. Indeed, it is perfectly possible for a puppy to enter the Open class, but as the class is open to 'all dogs of the breeds . . .' it must also be borne in mind that Champions can enter this class too, and however well behaved and good a specimen your puppy is, he is frankly unlikely to win among Champions because of his lack of maturity. Especially in the long-coated breeds, it can be very embarrassing for a new exhibitor to walk proudly into the ring with a six-month-old youngster on his very first outing, only to be surrounded by a class full of the breed's very best dogs, all of which are absolutely dripping in coat. So save yourself the embarrassment.

If you have, for example, an eight-month-old puppy which is still eligible for Minor Puppy, there is no reason at all why you shouldn't enter him also in a Puppy class and, if he is eligible, perhaps also a Maiden or Novice class, but just keep in your mind that the higher the class the stiffer the competition is likely to be. In any event, it would be unwise to tire him by entering him in too many classes; I think three should be the absolute maximum, especially for a youngster.

As you become more and more involved in your chosen breed you will also become aware of what is and what is not considered 'proper'. As was mentioned, technically a dog which has never won a first prize can be entered in the Open class or, for the sake of example, the Post Graduate class. In some breeds it is considered acceptable for a dog which has not yet won many first prizes to be entered in Post Graduate, or even a higher class, whereas in other breeds such an entry would be frowned upon. In some breeds, especially the larger breeds which are slower to mature, it is considered correct that a dog should win his way out of the classes so that if he has won only three first prizes he should not, in the eyes of other exhibitors at least, enter Post Graduate unless there is no lower class scheduled for which he is eligible. But, having said that, you need only abide by Kennel Club rules so the decision really rests with you.

## Entry in Any Variety classes

There is occasionally some confusion about entry in such classes. It is a Kennel Club rule that if there are one or more classes scheduled for a particular breed, an exhibit of that breed must be entered in a breed class if he is to be entered in an Any Variety class. It is not possible just to enter your dog in an AV class and ignore the breed classes. After all, if people were not to enter their dogs in the classes scheduled for their breed, sooner or later classes would be taken off the show schedule because they would not be a viable proposition. There is, though, an exception regarding puppies. If there are only adult classes scheduled for your breed you are at liberty to enter your puppy in Any Variety Puppy classes without being obliged to enter him also in a breed class. The reason for this is that he would be up against mature dogs in his breed class, thereby making the competition a little unfair. In such a situation you could not, however, miss the breed classes and go into an adult Any Variety class.

## The entry form

When you have decided which classes to enter you will need to fill in the entry form, which is usually to be found as a pull-out page inside the schedule. The form is fairly explicit so you should have no difficulty in completing it, but do be sure to print everything clearly, preferably in block capitals, for it is from these forms that

SHOW *

PLEASE USE SEPARATE FORM FOR EACH BREED OR OWNER

Entries Close: *

Entry Fees *

Will be held under Kennel Club Rules and Show Regulations

Breeds entered
1 ................
2 ................
3 ................

INSTRUCTIONS   This form must be used by one person only, (or partnership)
Use one line only for each dog. The name of the dog and all the details as recorded with the Kennel Club must be given on the entry form. If an error is made the dog may be disqualified by the Committee of the Kennel Club. All dogs must be REGISTERED at the Kennel Club and if a Registered dog has changed ownership the TRANSFER must be registered before date of Show. A Puppy under 6 months old cannot be exhibited.
When entering more than one breed or variety, use if possible, a separate form for each. On no account will entries be accepted without fees.
Writing MUST BE IN INK OR INDELIBLE PENCIL
(On no account will entries be accepted without fees)

For Secretary's use only

| REGISTERED NAME OF DOG | BREED | SEX D or B | Full Date of Birth | BREEDER | SIRE (BLOCK LETTERS) | DAM (BLOCK LETTERS) | To be entered in Classes numbered |
|---|---|---|---|---|---|---|---|
| | | | | | | | |
| | | | | | | | |
| | | | | | | | |
| | | | | | | | |
| | | | | | | | |

ONE LINE FOR EACH DOG. PUT CLASSES IN NUMERICAL ORDER & CHECK ALL DETAILS BEFORE POSTING

DECLARATION
I undertake to abide by the Rules and Regulations of the Kennel Club and of this Show and I declare that the dogs entered have not contracted or been knowingly exposed to any infectious or contagious disease during the six weeks prior to exhibition and I will not exhibit them if they incur such risks between now and the day of the Show.
I affirm that the dogs which will be exhibited will only be prepared for exhibition in accordance with the requirements of Kennel Club Regulations for the Preparation of Dogs for Exhibition F.
I further declare that, I believe to the best of my knowledge that the dogs are not liable to disqualification under Kennel Club Show Regulations.

Usual Signature of Owner(s) ................   Date ................

Note: Dog entered in breach of Kennel Club Show Regulations are liable to disqualification whether or not the owner was aware of the breach.

© Permission is granted to Societies and Dog Training Clubs registered with the Kennel Club to reproduce copies.

BLOCK LETTERS

Name of Owner(s)
ADDRESS

Telephone No.

Entries and Fees which MUST BE PREPAID to be sent to:
*

Please complete these slips – do not detach

NAME
ADDRESS

Breeds entered (in schedule order, please)
(1) ........................
(2) ........................
(3) ........................
ENTER NAME OF DOG HERE

NAME
ADDRESS

NAME
ADDRESS

Figure 1   The bare outline of a show schedule. Sections marked * are printed in by each individual show society; you will need to complete the rest

catalogue information is compiled and printed. Printers do make mistakes sometimes, but if you have not written your dog's name clearly the blame really must rest with you if it appears incorrectly spelt in the catalogue. In the column regarding sex, D of course stands for dog and B for bitch (one tends to use dog and bitch far more frequently than male and female with reference to the canine species). Take care that the date of birth you are listing is accurate, and when giving the breeder's name it is wise to use an initial, for obvious reasons: Mrs G.J. Jones will give catalogue readers much more information than just Mrs Jones, for it is possible that there are other breeders with the same surname.

When listing the numbers of the classes in which you wish to enter your dog, do be sure to keep a record on the schedule which you will retain for reference. Many a time does one witness an exhibitor walking into the wrong class with a dog because she thought she had entered a different class and did not check in the catalogue. Even worse are the unfortunate cases when exhibitors arrive at shows with the wrong dogs, or perhaps arrive on Hound day when their Utility breed was judged the previous day. Believe me, these things happen with much more frequency than you might imagine!

Always be sure that your cheque is made out correctly and that you put your own name, address and breed of dog entered on the back of the cheque. Post-dated cheques are not acceptable and, as it says on the form, 'on no account will entries be accepted without fees'. Finally, you have to sign the declaration as given in the bottom left-hand corner of the form, and I would urge you to read this carefully for it would be totally unfair to other exhibitors if you were to take your dog along to a show in the knowledge that he had been in contact with an infectious or contagious disease within the stipulated six-week period prior to the show. You are also signing to say that your dog will be prepared for exhibition under KC Regulations and you will find that 'Regulations for the Preparation of Dogs for Exhibition F' are contained either in the schedule or on the back of the entry form. Do please read it so that you don't, albeit unwittingly, use an unsuitable substance in preparing your dog's coat. Keep in mind, too, that not all coat preparations for sale at shows are necessarily suitable for use in accordance with this rule.

Most Show Secretaries will acknowledge receipt of your entry if you enclose a stamped addressed postcard, but in any event, in the case of General Championship shows passes will be sent out to exhibitors a few days before the date of the show. If, by three working days before the show, you have not received your passes you should ring the Secretary to confirm that everything is in order. If the passes have been sent out but appear to have been delayed in the post, don't panic; when you get to the show have a word with the gate attendant to explain what has happened. You will most probably have to pay a fee to enter the showground but if you report immediately to the Secretary's office you should find that this will be reimbursed. Obviously this will cause you a little delay, so if you know that your passes have gone astray allow yourself a few extra minutes so that you still have plenty of time to be judged in your class.

## The cost of entering a show

If you have sent for some schedules you will already have discovered that the cost of entries differs according to the show society and the type of show. In general, Championship shows are substantially more expensive to enter than Limited and Open shows, the cost of the first entry with each dog at the former presently being roughly £10 whereas at a Limited or Open show one rarely has to pay more than about £3.50 and sometimes even less. At some shows the cost of the catalogue is included in the entry fee, but on some entry forms you will find a section stating that you can book your catalogue if paid for in advance; on these occasions it is not always possible to buy a catalogue on the day of the show, so if you want one don't forget to order. At other shows catalogues are simply sold at the show.

One of the reasons why General Championship shows are more expensive to enter is that all dogs have to be benched, and in the end it is the exhibitor who has to cover the cost of the benching. However, specialist breed club shows are usually a little less expensive than General Championship shows (i.e. those for all breeds), especially if the club has obtained from the Kennel Club an exemption from benching, which is often possible. Indeed, I would always recommend that the newer exhibitor enters as many breed club shows as possible, for they are a fine opportunity to exhibit with relatively little expense and to meet many of the breed's major enthusiasts and their dogs. In your very early days in the show-ring you can easily spend a great deal of money entering General Championship shows before you have actually determined whether or not your dog is in with a chance of

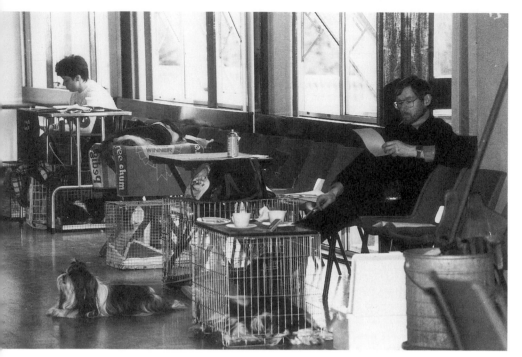

*The organisers of this Breed Club Show have allowed plenty of space for grooming and equipment. Enjoying a cup of tea by the mop bucket is not unknown at dog shows!*

winning. It would certainly be cheaper to restrict yourself to showing up to Open show level and at breed club shows until you feel that your dog is of high enough quality to stand a fair chance at Championship level. Sadly, there are a great many dogs which are dragged around to Championship shows up and down the country with very little chance of getting in the cards, except under an undiscerning judge or in a class with a very low entry. It must cost owners of such dogs a small fortune – but I suppose they enjoy the day out!

Once you have paid the initial entry fee for each dog, the cost of entering the same dog in a second or subsequent class is very much less, perhaps just another £1 for example. However, apart from the entry fee you will also presumably want to buy a catalogue, which can cost up to a couple of pounds; you may also have to pay a car-parking fee or even a caravan fee if you are one of those fortunate people who can take off with your caravan for a night or so without having to worry about other dogs left at home.

Most of the major Championship shows have facilities for caravans either on or very near to the showground, and although I have never experienced the thrills of caravanning at dog shows, I gather that everyone has a wonderful time and that it is an excellent way of meeting like-minded folk.

Then, of course, there are the petrol costs to consider; many people team up together to share the expense and to avoid the monotony of driving alone if they are travelling a long distance. The coach is an alternative means of transport and in those all-important schedules you will find details of people who organise coach journeys to each specific show from various parts of the country, with pick-up points *en route*. Do check with the organisers as to how they arrange the trip, for one often has to book a seat per person and a seat per dog or dogs, depending upon how much space is required. Coach trips can be another good way of meeting people, especially if you are travelling alone, and many coach enthusiasts have some hilarious stories to tell about their experiences. The disadvantage, I feel, is that the coaches usually leave as soon as their passengers' judging is complete, so one doesn't get a great deal of time to look around the show and

*Special coach trips to shows are organised from all parts of the country with special pick-up points* en route

study some of the other breeds and Group competition. If, however, one of the passengers is fortunate enough to win Best of Breed, the coach usually waits for them to compete in the Group.

It is usually well worth the bother of taking along a flask of coffee and a packed lunch, especially to some of the lovely outdoor shows, for frequently the cost of food at shows is high and the selection not always as wide as one might wish – added to which, there are frequently some very long queues which can be infuriating if one is starving but anxious not to miss a particular class!

All in all, dog showing is certainly not a cheap hobby, particularly when one considers that, apart from the actual show expenses, you have to buy show equipment, feed and house your dogs, pay veterinary bills and purchase at least one canine newspaper each week. Nonetheless, if you become 'hooked', as so many of us do, you will find some way of covering those expenses, even if it means giving up some other little luxury in order to do so.

## Classification of the various breeds

In the UK, breeds are divided into six groups. The Hound group, Gundog group and Terrier group are classified as Sporting breeds and the Utility group, Working group and Toy group are Non-Sporting breeds. Take care when you are entering classes other than those for your specific breed that you are sure of your classification; an Afghan Hound, for example, would be AV Hound or AV Sporting, but a Keeshond is classified under Utility and so would be eligible for AV Utility or AV Non-Sporting. Also, if you are entering a show which spans more than one day you must know on which day you need to attend, although in the case of General Championship shows this will be shown on the pass which is sent to you prior to the show. The following list will, I hope, be of both interest and assistance, for when your own breed has been judged it is always absorbing to watch some of the other breeds if you have time.

HOUND GROUP

| | |
|---|---|
| Afghan Hound | Beagle |
| Basenji | Bloodhound |
| Basset Hound | Borzoi |
| Basset Fauve de Bretagne | Dachsbrake |

Dachshund (Long-Haired)
Dachshund (Min. Long-Haired)
Dachshund (Smooth-Haired)
Dachshund (Min. Smooth-Haired)
Dachshund (Wire-Haired)
Dachshund (Min. Wire-Haired)
Deerhound
Elkhound
Finnish Spitz
Foxhound
Grand Bleu de Gascogne (Imp Reg)
Greyhound
Hamiltonstovare

Ibizan Hound
Irish Wolfhound
Norwegian Lundehund (Imp Reg)
Otterhound
Petit Basset Griffon Vendene
Pharaoh Hound
Portuguese Warren Hound
   (Imp Reg)
Rhodesian Ridgeback
Saluki
Sloughi
Swiss Laufhund (Jura) (Imp Reg)
Whippet

### GUNDOG GROUP

Brittany
Drentse Partridge Dog
English Setter
German Long-Haired Pointer
   (Imp Reg)
German Short-Haired Pointer
German Wire-Haired Pointer
Gordon Setter
Hungarian Visla
Hungarian Wire-Haired Visla
Irish Red & White Setter
Irish Setter
Italian Spinone
Kooikerhundje (Imp Reg)
Large Munsterlander
Pointer
Pointing Wire-haired Griffon

Retriever (Chesapeake Bay)
Retriever (Curly-Coated)
Retriever (Flat-Coated)
Retriever (Golden)
Retriever (Labrador)
Small Munsterlander
Spaniel (American Cocker)
Spaniel (American Water)
   (Imp Reg)
Spaniel (Clumber)
Spaniel (Cocker)
Spaniel (English Springer)
Spaniel (Field)
Spaniel (Irish Water)
Spaniel (Sussex)
Spaniel (Welsh Springer)
Weimaraner

### TERRIER GROUP

Airedale Terrier
Australian Terrier
Bedlington Terrier
Border Terrier
Bull Terrier
Bull Terrier (Miniature)
Cairn Terrier
Dandie Dinmont Terrier
Fox Terrier (Smooth)
Fox Terrier (Wire)
Glen of Imal Terrier
Irish Terrier

Kerry Blue Terrier
Lakeland Terrier
Manchester Terrier
Norfolk Terrier
Norwich Terrier
Scottish Terrier
Sealyham Terrier
Skye Terrier
Soft-Coated Wheaten Terrier
Staffordshire Bull Terrier
Welsh Terrier
West Highland White Terrier

### UTILITY GROUP

Boston Terrier
Bulldog
Canaan Dog
Chow Chow
Dalmatian
French Bulldog
German Spitz (Klein)
German Spitz (Mittel)
Iceland Dog (Imp Reg)
Japanese Akita
Japanese Shiba Inu (Imp Reg)
Japanese Spitz
Keeshond
Leonberger
Lhasa Apso
Mexican Hairless (Imp Reg)
Miniature Schnauzer
Poodle (Standard)
Poodle (Miniature)
Poodle (Toy)
Schipperke
Schnauzer
Shar-Pei
Shih Tzu
Tibetan Spaniel
Tibetan Terrier

### WORKING GROUP

Alaskan Malamute
Anatolian Shepherd Dog
Australian Cattle Dog
Austrailian Kelpie
Bearded Collie
Beauceron (Imp Reg)
Belgian Shepherd Dog
(Groenendale)
Belgian Shepherd Dog (Laekenois)
Belgian Shepherd Dog (Malinois)
Belgian Shepherd Dog (Turvueren)
Bernese Mountain Dog
Border Collie
Bouvier des Flandres
Boxer
Briard
Bullmastiff
Collie (Rough)
Collie (Smooth)
Continental Landseer (ECT)
(Imp Reg)
Dobermann
Eskimo Dog
Estrela Mountain Dog
German Shepherd Dog (Alsatian)
Giant Schnauzer
Great Dane
Hovawart
Hungarian Kuvasz
Hungarian Puli
Komondor
Lancashire Heeler
Maremma Sheepdog
Mastiff
Neapolitan Mastiff
Newfoundland
Norwegian Buhund
Old English Sheepdog
Pinscher
Polish Lowland Sheepdog
(Imp Reg)
Portuguese Water Dog
Pyrenean Mountain Dog
Pyrenean Sheepdog (Imp Reg)
Rottweiler
St Bernard
Samoyed
Shetland Sheepdog
Siberian Husky
Swedish Lapphund (Imp Reg)
Swedish Vallhund
Tibetan Mastiff
Welsh Corgie (Cardigan)
Welsh Corgie (Pembroke)

TOY GROUP

Affenpinscher
Australian Silky Terrier
Bichon Frise
Bolognese (Imp Reg)
Cavalier King Charles Spaniel
Chihuahua (Long Coat)
Chihuahua (Smooth Coat)
Chinese Crested
English Toy Terrier (Black & Tan)
Griffon Bruxellois
Italian Greyhound

Japanese Chin
King Charles Spaniel
Lowchen (Little Lion Dog)
Maltese
Miniature Pinscher
Papillon
Pekingese
Pomeranian
Pug
Yorkshire Terrier

# 4

# Equipment for you and your dog

Some breeds need more special show equipment than others, the primary divisions coming between the large and the small breeds, and between those which are long-coated and those which are not. You may also find some difference in what you need to take depending upon whether or not the show is benched and if there is likely to be ample room at the venue.

## Large dogs

If yours is a long-legged, short-coated breed you will probably need little more than the minimum of grooming equipment, a show lead, a benching chain and something comfortable for your dog to lie on while on the bench. If you are on your way to one of the outdoor shows which is not benched you may find it useful to take along a stake to which your dog can be tethered while you sit with him by the ring-side, although a dog tethered to a stake in the ground should, of course, never be left unattended both for his own safety and for that of passers-by and their dogs. We will now look at these various pieces of equipment in a little more detail.

*Leads*   As you walk your dog into the venue you will need to see that he is secure and will find it safer for him to be on his normal, somewhat sturdy collar and lead, the one you use all the time when he goes out for walks. This, however, will most probably be a little too heavy to use in the show-ring where it is usually quite safe for you to use a slip lead as you will be concentrating one hundred per cent on your dog so he is unlikely to escape. To use a slip lead on an excited dog walking through the showground car park, while you are loaded up with benching blankets and picnic baskets, can lead to disaster if he doubles back to play with a group of dogs approaching from behind. Again, the size of your breed and, in some breeds, fashion in the ring will determine what type of show lead will best suit your dog, but you will find an enormously wide range available at virtually every large show. Something you want to avoid is a lead which is so long that you are likely to have yards of it hanging down; it should be short enough to be concealed in your hand while you are exhibiting your dog.

*Benching chain*　This is a necessity if you are attending a benched show and your dog is not a breed which is kept in a crate at the show. The weight of the chain should be selected in accordance with the size of your dog, and its length can be adjusted at the point where you attach the clip of the lead. The lead used while your dog is on the bench must be of the normal type rather than the slip variety. You will find a loop attached to the back corner of the show-bench and it is to this that you attach the benching chain, taking care that you have adjusted the chain to such a length that your dog cannot simply step off the bench – although the chain must not be so short that he is over-restricted. It is rarely possible to buy benching chains at ordinary pet stores, so if you don't already have one when you go to your first benched show, make your first port of call one of the major stand-holders, who will undoubtedly be able to fix you up before you and your dog get to the bench.

*Stake*　You are not likely to need a stake at a benched show for it is a KC rule that dogs must be on their benches most of the time when they are not actually in the show-ring. However, a stake can be very useful if you like to go along to the unbenched outdoor summer shows where you can sit by the rings with your dog to watch the judging. Provided they are put into the ground securely, stakes are a good way of keeping your dog with you while freeing your hands to eat your sandwiches. It is often possible to buy stakes at normal pet shops (as they are useful in the garden and when visiting friends, too), but should you have difficulty in obtaining one, like most things they can be purchased from one of the trade stands at major shows.

*

Not all dogs, however, are long-legged and short-coated. Other types have more problems (or attributes, whichever way you like to look at it) and therefore need more equipment. If yours is a large breed with a profuse coat, you may have no difficulty in getting into the showground looking perfectly spick and span on a fine dry day, but if the rain pours down and turns the already sodden grass into a quagmire, you will require some extra equipment with which to protect your dog. You will need a raincoat and, most probably, a grooming table. It is true that there are now some very large dog crates on the market, but under normal circumstances these are rather too cumbersome to transport, and in any event a very large crate will not fit on a bench.

*Raincoats*   These come in all shapes and sizes and the salesperson will usually be able to fix you up with the right size if you tell him the breed of dog and give an indication of its height at the

*This Afghan Hound's wardrobe includes not only a raincoat but boots too!*

*Afghan Hound owners especially like to keep their dogs in snoods as pictured here. This is a good way of preventing the long ear fringes from getting soiled*

shoulder. The raincoat, made of waterproof material and available in a variety of colours, covers most parts of the anatomy, with a convenient space left under the tail so that your dog can still carry out his normal bodily functions, even in the pouring rain. Nevertheless, it is wise to let your dog get used to his new attire before he goes to a show, for sometimes a dog is reluctant to spend a penny in his new outfit, and when he first does so it is not unknown for him to miss his aim and end up with one unpleasantly wet inside leg!

Optional extras come in the form of rain hats and rain shoes (I wouldn't go so far as to call them wellingtons) but I have never had much success in keeping these on. I suspect that other people experience just as much difficulty as I do, for it is quite a common sight to see a dog walking into a show with shoes on three feet, the fourth having mysteriously disappeared. I have found that a much more sensible arrangement is to use eight pop-socks and four polythene bags: on each foot put a sock, followed by a polythene bag and then another sock. You may need to keep hitching them up a bit on the way into the showground, and, indeed, your large hairy beast may look rather more comical than elegant, but at least his feet will be dry. On days when it is not raining but the ground is wet underfoot, this rig-out is very useful – although I was once almost refused entry to a Championship show by an obstreperous man on the gate who insisted that my hairy black pop-socked Afghan was not a pedigree dog!

*Grooming table*   If you are going to show your large, long-coated dog seriously you will sooner or later want to invest in a grooming table which you can take to shows, for it is not easy to groom a dog to perfection on the floor. Again, you will find that those invaluable trade stands at major shows have a good selection available. Such tables are quite expensive but a good-quality one will give you many years' valuable service. Those which I feel to be the most practical have a non-slip surface, are collapsible and can be wheeled along with the aid of a sturdy handle which doubles as a support when the table is erected. Many also act as a trolley, and such a table can, of course, also be used as a grooming table in your own home, so it really is a worthwhile investment.

# Smaller dogs

Now we come to the smaller breeds which, whether long- or short-coated, are likely to require a crate. If yours is one of the Toy breeds you will find that at benched shows your bench is automatically fitted with a crate. If, however, you have a small breed which is not classified as a Toy, there will be no crate incorporated in the benching facility, and unless you wish to leave your dog attached by a benching chain (something I consider very unwise for a small breed) you will have to purchase a crate of some sort. You will also need some means of conveying your crate to the bench, for which you can use either one of the collapsible tables described above or a trolley on which your crate will fit. Indeed, it is now possible to purchase a crate and trolley combined which looks super and seems very practical, although it does have the disadvantage that you cannot take it to pieces and the crate therefore does not fit on to the bench when required.

*Crates*   These come in a variety of sizes, but you must choose one in which your dog can stand up, turn round and lie down in comfort. Having said that, if you are going to need to use the crate on your dog's bench then it should not be too large to fit. Some crates are collapsible; the cheaper ones frequently are not, but I

*The trade stands are invaluable. You will find a good selection of equipment including crates, grooming tables and hair-dryers as shown here*

do think it is worth investing in a collapsible one if possible because, as well as being practical, they are usually more sturdily made. Some are automatically fitted with a tray in the base, but if not, a tray can often be purchased as an optional extra; this is a very useful addition for it undoubtedly provides a slightly more comfortable surface for the dog to sit on, can be wiped down easily and avoids the danger of your dog's feet slipping through the holes. Be sure, too, that you select a crate which has a good tight fastening so that you feel confident your dog cannot release the mechanism himself. You will need something with which to line the base of the crate – a piece of Vetbed or similar, cut to the correct size, would certainly be the most suitable for it can so easily be washed between shows.

It is possible also to buy a cover for your crate; this will be made of waterproof fabric and will often have a transparent front flap with a zip for easy access to the crate. I know that many people handy with a needle make their own crate covers, which is quite a cost saving, and if you are accomplished in this area (which some of us are not), the pattern is quite simple.

In theory you could carry your small dog into the show under one arm with your collapsible crate in your free hand, but in practice that is more easily said than done, especially if you have decided to take along a flask of coffee and a picnic as well as your grooming equipment and the piece of Vetbed with which to line the crate. I think you will very soon reach the conclusion that a trolley of some sort would be a wise investment.

*Trolleys and trolley-tables*    A trolley-table, as described above, is a very useful piece of apparatus for you can erect your crate, put your dog inside and trolley all your goods and chattels into the showground; once at your bench you can install dog and crate on

*When the show is over your trolley and crate will be of great assistance in helping you to get your dogs and many purchases back to the car. This exhibitor's piece of equipment is a trolley and crate combined*

the bench and erect the trolley as a table on which to groom – taking care, of course, not to block the gangway by doing so.

An alternative is to have a simple trolley, which has the advantage of not being as heavy as a trolley-table and is therefore probably more suitable for anyone who does not wish to lift heavy weights or who is likely to be travelling alone to shows. Be sure that the trolley is large enough to take your crate and make sure that everything is balanced evenly when loading up, to avoid it tipping over en route. Some adjustable trolleys are now available which can be expanded or enlarged to fit exactly to the size of your crate. The disadvantage of using just a trolley is that once at your bench you have no grooming table of your own, but the problem is not insurmountable. If you use either a piece of board cut to size or a good, firm, thick rubber car mat, this can be placed on top of the crate and used as a base upon which to groom. It is also possible to purchase a special 'table-top' for the purpose.

*Elasticated straps*   These do need a special mention of their own because they are a most essential piece of equipment for anyone using trolleys and crates. If you don't already have some, buy two or three from a garage on the way to your first show, for without them your journey from vehicle to bench will take twice as long because you can almost guarantee that things will fall off en route. When I recently drove away leaving my straps on the roof of the car, I was glad to discover that one of the trade stands at major shows had started to sell them. Presumably elastic straps have now, at long last, firmly established themselves as standard pieces of canine equipment.

Now you have all your equipment for your dog, but have you thought about equipment for yourself and your own attire?

# Other equipment and personal dress

First of all it is necessary to bear in mind that dog shows take place in all seasons and therefore in all weathers. Winter shows have to be scheduled to take place in an indoor venue, but organisers of summer shows usually like to arrange for the show-rings to be outdoors, although there is always a facility for indoor judging in the case of wet weather, perhaps in a hall or, more frequently, in a tent. Equestrian centres, empty cowsheds and even car auction rooms also play their part as indoor venues, and as a result one has to be prepared for all types of conditions underfoot. After one or two years on the show circuit you will get to know the venues and the conditions you are likely to encounter at each, but nevertheless the weather can always play havoc with the best-laid plans. It is not impossible for one of the early summer shows to be carpeted in snow, while on the other hand you can go wrapped up in your warmest gear to a winter show only to find that your breed is benched next to one of those enormous, noisy industrial blow heaters which bellow out almost unbearable heat. The possibilities are endless, and you are certainly in for a challenge! Also consider that some shows have ample seating arrangements whereas others do not, so if you want to sit somewhere other than on your bench you will need to take along a picnic chair or something similar. It is always a sensible idea to keep an umbrella in the boot of your car: it can be used not only to keep off the rain but also as a parasol to keep the sun off your dog while grooming or waiting to go in the ring. A towel is also an essential piece of equipment with a variety of uses.

Let us now look in detail at your own personal dress. It has to be practical but must also be suitable for the type of dog that you show. You would, for example, look somewhat incongruous if you were to teeter round the ring with your Deerhound wearing high heels and a tight mini-skirt; sensible shoes and a wax jacket would be far more likely to help you pass as 'one of us'. Whatever the venue, you do not wish to wear shoes which 'clunk' round the ring as you move your dog; high heels and sling-backs are definitely out at dog shows, for not only can they put off your own dog but they can worry the dog in front of you when he hears the noisy clip-clop of your heels following him round the ring, so such shoes are not designed to make you popular with the other exhibitors. Also avoid noisy or dangly jewellery, for what might seem perfectly practical at any other social event might just distract your dog (or your neighbour's dog) or, worse still, get caught up in his coat so that you are obliged to spend time disentangling yourselves when you should be presenting him to the judge. Another no-no is money jingling in your pockets, so please take heed. Talking of accessories, it is generally not a good idea to wear a hat in the ring, partly for fear of it blowing or falling off and distracting all and sundry, but also, in the case of wide-brimmed hats, because shadows can be created which might be momentarily off-putting for your dog. Indeed, many a table dog has shown a surprised reaction when a judge has bent over in a large hat, so do think twice before donning your headgear.

Women should remember that when showing one often has to bend over – stocking tops and layers of lily-white flesh six inches above the knee are not pretty sights for the ring-side crowd. I always think it is a good idea to dress in layers so that you can either add or take off a layer according to the weather. Bear in mind that you will often be arriving at a show in the early hours of the morning when it is cool but that by midday the sun can be beating down on both you and your dog, so do be prepared for extremes of temperature. A light-weight waterproof which rolls into a tiny ball can also come in handy at times, especially at a summer show in teeming rain when the loo is located at the opposite end of the showground, and you would be well advised to keep a pair of wellingtons permanently in the corner of your car boot, for car parks can be very muddy, especially if you are exhibiting on the second or third day of the show so that the ground has been well churned up by vehicles before the day of your arrival.

You also need to give thought to the colour and style of your own clothes. With certain breeds no one seems to bother about setting off their dog, and the example I gave above regarding Deerhounds really is true: it seems to be acceptable for the grey colour of the dog to blend in with the dark green of a wax jacket. But such breeds are the exception rather than the rule. It is generally to your advantage to choose a colour which will show off your dog's outline; you will not, for example, do justice to your dog if you wear a cream skirt or trousers when showing a white dog, or indeed dark maroon clothes with a dark-coloured dog. You also want to avoid large patterns on your skirt or trousers for they can cause an optical illusion so that the judge sees the dog as a slightly different shape at a quick glance. Some colours also look quite different in the artificial light of an indoor venue. Indeed, I have been caught out myself by wearing a colourful striped skirt when showing a black dog – it looked a super contrast outside but apparently, much to my surprise, my dog simply blended into my skirt indoors.

On the subject of skirts, be careful not to wear one which is too full so that it blows about, for this particular type of skirt has a habit of blowing directly into a dog's face, obstructing the dog's vision and often completely obliterating the judge's view of the dog as it moves towards him. On the other hand, tight skirts are clearly impractical and trousers need to be roomy enough for you to bend down and to move your dog around the ring, possibly at a fairly rapid speed. You will find that you learn from your mistakes. I vividly recall one of my most embarrassing moments in the ring when the inside seam of my trousers split as the judge was going over my Afghan. It was a very large class which seemed to last for ever, and as the judge moved us round and round the ring I felt the split grow and grow until it was right down to my knee. I won the class and the next one too, but I hope the judge was honourable enough to have made his decision entirely on the merits of my dog! It took me ages to obtain a needle and cotton with which to do a repair job afterwards, so I now highly recommend keeping a little sewing kit handy when you go to a show.

In some breeds exhibitors like to wear little aprons with pockets in which they keep all manner of things, including titbits with which to bait their dogs in the ring. If you, too, decide to wear an apron, make sure that it is always spotlessly clean so that it does not give you a shabby appearance. You will often find some very attractive ones for sale at shows, sometimes depicting your chosen breed on the pockets.

Fashions change and tastes vary, but basically it is worth while trying at least to look neat and tidy. After all, you may have spent many hours preparing your dog to go to the show so you don't want to spoil the overall appearance you are wishing to create by going into the ring looking like a bundle of rubbish yourself. Some exhibitors manage to look immaculate from 8 a.m. until 4 p.m., with a clean, tidy suit (often in a pale beige colour!) and not a hair on their head out of place. While I admire such people, I think it is more important to be practical; as long as you dress to suit your dog, I suspect you will find that if you are simply clean, tidy and comfortable, you will enjoy your day all the more.

# Getting to the show

## *By car*

If you intend to travel by car, do be sure that your vehicle is roadworthy and that all essentials such as petrol, oil, water and tyre pressures have been checked; starting off in the early hours of the morning with only a drop of petrol in the tank could mean that you miss your class because you have been caught out waiting for a petrol station to open at 7 a.m. It's happened to me and I can tell you that it's infuriating. Pack your car the night before the show, for you can be almost certain that if you leave it until the morning it will take you longer than anticipated and you will eventually set off at least a quarter of an hour later than planned.

Plan your route at least the day before the show so that you don't underestimate the time the journey will take, and make sure that you know exactly where the show venue is. Remember that just because a show society is called by a certain place-name it does not necessarily mean that the show is held in that town; it may be a good few miles away. And if you are going to a show which is to be held in a village with a name that is unknown to you, check the spelling very carefully and be sure that there is not another village of the same name in another county. It can, and does, happen! Most show schedules include directions to the venue but do be sure to have a map in the car as well, just in case you happen not to approach by the same route as the person who went to the trouble of drawing the map or writing the directions.

When you do finally set off I would strongly suggest that your dog does not wear a lead in the car, as some have been known to get tangled up in them and even strangle themselves when left alone for a short while. It is, however, a good idea to keep a collar on him for this will give details of your address in the unhappy event of there being an accident. Many people like their dogs to travel to shows in their crates, and from the safety point of view there are arguments both for and against this, so I must leave you to make up your own mind in this regard. Certainly many dogs seem to be more comfortable travelling in a confined space rather than being left to roam about in the back of an estate car; in fact, the latter can tend to make the most car-happy dog sick. Tempting though it is, it is not wise to allow your puppy to sit with you on the passenger seat when travelling to his first show, even though your intention may be just to reassure him, for you will find that if you begin by letting him travel in this way he will come to expect it and may give you a very noisy journey when the time comes for him to be relegated to the back.

If you are going to a Championship show with a dog puppy (dogs are always judged before bitches and in breed competition puppies are always judged first in each sex) you should aim to arrive at the venue at least an hour before judging is due to commence. If the show is on a week-day you must make allowances for meeting traffic if you have to drive through towns

*Packing the car to travel home from a show requires even greater skill than loading up prior to the journey there!*

and cities; also keep in the back of your mind that there may well be a queue of cars waiting to get into the showground if you are arriving about an hour before judging like almost every other exhibitor. Car parks, too, can be located a good distance from the benches and rings, and it will probably take you a good few minutes to unload the car, especially if you have to contend with a trolley and cage. Upon arrival it is always a good idea to mark on the schedule (this can later be transferred to the catalogue which you will keep) the journey time, including any stops for a cup of coffee or a stretch of several pairs of legs en route; you will find this very helpful when planning your journey for the next show at the same venue. Looking ahead, at the end of the day it is all too easy to forget where you parked the car so make a mental note of your location as you unload and walk to the entrance gate. Remember that there is often more than one entrance and that the owner of the large red van which was conveniently parked next to you and has been pinpointed as your landmark may decide to go home before you. Oh, and before you leave the car, do make sure that your entry passes and catalogue voucher (if applied for) are handy to give in when you get to the entrance; don't leave them in the glove compartment of the car.

## By coach

We briefly discussed coach travel in the last chapter when talking about cost. Special coach services are run from many parts of the country and the organiser usually plans the route with various predestined stops along the way so that passengers can be picked up sometimes many miles from the starting point. If you are travelling with a friend you may decide that your small dog can sit with you on a lap, but remember that the trip you are making is probably going to be a long one and you may be well advised to lash out a few extra pounds for another seat. Depending on the journey involved the coach may well set off in the middle of the night, so do take this, and your journey to the pick-up point, into consideration before you make your booking. Often one of the designated pick-up points is at a motorway service station, which sounds very convenient. But can you park your car there for almost a whole day, or if someone drops you off there so as to avoid leaving the car, can they get back on to the motorway to travel home in the opposite direction? Check these things, too, before you make your final decision as to the mode of transport you intend to use.

# Other practicalities

If your dog has had a long journey it is highly likely that he will want to relieve himself before he gets to the designated 'exercise area', so do make sure that you have a useful piece of equipment with which to scoop up if necessary. Proper dog scoops are available but it is just as convenient to carry a polythene bag in your pocket, ideally with a tissue as well, and with a deft flick of the wrist the deposit can be removed and a knot tied in the end of the bag so that it can be conveniently disposed of at the first available and suitable receptacle. Don't be like those people who walk on regardless, pretending that it wasn't their dog who did it.

Just think of the mess which could be avoided if everyone cleaned up after their dogs; it is really the only honourable thing to do. Some show societies are actually kind enough to make arrangements so that each exhibitor is provided with a scoop, in which case please make sure you use it if necessary. It is worthy of mention here that many a good venue has been lost to a show society purely because of thoughtless exhibitors who have not cleaned up after their dogs.

At some point you will be confronted by a gate official; this may be at the entrance to the car park (in which case you will probably have to give in your passes at that point) but it is more likely to be at the entrance to the exhibition and tenting area itself. At Open shows it is rare for entrance passes to be sent out, but for Championship shows (except many breed club shows) you will have received your pass through the post. The number of passes you receive will depend upon the number of dogs you are exhibiting, but if you have only one dog, any travelling companions will most probably have to pay a fee to get into the show. This is usually something in the region of £1 to £2 but can be substantially more at the large agricultural shows where visitors will also be at liberty to view the pigs, goats and cattle if they choose to do so. Take care that you retain the appropriate portion of your pass (you usually give in just one section) for it will be needed by the gateman when you leave. This is in order to keep a check on dogs leaving the venue; people who went in with one dog should, of course, go out with one, not two. A word of advice for those friends and relations who may decide to visit the show with you; only dogs which are entered for the show are allowed into the showground, so they should not take along their own pets 'just for the ride'. A few of the outdoor shows do now have a tent outside the showground where visiting dogs can be accommodated, but this by no means applies to all shows and dogs should never be left in cars.

On a summer day it is surprising how quickly the heat builds up inside a car, even with the windows open, and it is now common practice for officials to patrol the car park to check that no dogs have been left in cars; if any are found in distress, strong action can be taken against the owner. Sadly, not a year seems to go by without some dogs dying of heat exhaustion in dog-show car parks; admittedly many of these belong to non-exhibiting visitors to the show, but not all exhibitors are exempt from blame themselves.

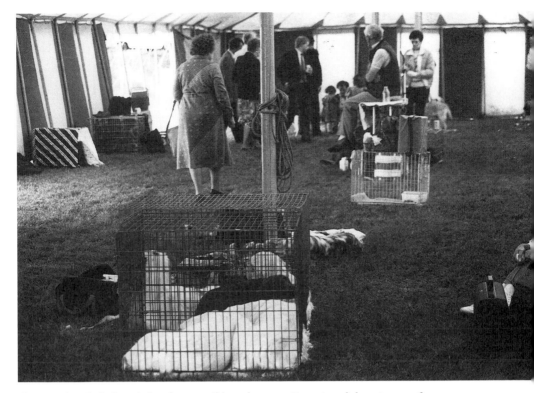

*At an unbenched show it is often possible to leave equipment and dogs in one of the wet weather tents such as this*

Although I hope that readers of this book are never likely to be guilty of leaving a dog in a car, the Kennel Club has given guidelines to organisers of shows as to how to deal with offending parties. It is considered that on a hot day the act of causing suffering to a dog as a result of being left in a car could be discreditable or prejudicial to the interests of the canine world. The Kennel Club recommends that wherever possible, evidence of suffering should be provided by a veterinary surgeon or an RSPCA official, but in the absence of such expert opinion the evidence of experienced and responsible dog owners will be acceptable. Show Secretaries and individuals are asked to make reports, where appropriate, so that offenders can be asked to account for their actions. It is recommended that when a dog is found in a distressed condition an announcement is made on a public address system, giving not only details of the dog involved but also the name of the owner if known, together with the make and registration number of the vehicle. If no action is taken within five to ten minutes a veterinary surgeon should decide whether the condition of the dog is such that another call can be put out. If the dog is in a distressed condition and there is no response, the Kennel Club states that a show official should then take 'appropriate action'.

Please, if you think enough of your dog to have bothered to read this book, don't be one of the few people at virtually every large summer show whose car number is read out over the loudspeakers.

Whatever the season, it goes without saying that you must have packed a drinking bowl for your dog. Ideally you should also take along a bottle of fresh water, but if you need to cut down on weight (or if you need a refill), water taps are always to be found at showgrounds; at outdoor shows they are usually located at strategic points near the tenting areas.

Once past the gateman your first port of call will be to the catalogue stand which is usually just inside the gate, so don't walk past it or you may have a long walk back. Depending upon the show society, you may have had the opportunity to pay for your catalogue when you made your entry, in which case you will have been sent a voucher which is exchanged for the appropriate catalogue on the day. At a few shows there are separate catalogues for each group so do be sure that if you have, for example, a Saluki, your catalogue is for the Hound group and not the Working group. Of course, you don't have to buy a catalogue, but I always feel lost without one. Especially if you are new to showing, your catalogue will be your bible for through this medium you will be able to find out who's who, who owns what and how the various dogs are bred. You will be able to mark up the prize-winners in the catalogue at the end of each class so that you have your own personal record of the dogs preferred by each judge under which you have exhibited. Catalogues take up a lot of storage space at home but they are well worth keeping. I once had a mammoth clear-out when I moved house, throwing away years and years of marked catalogues; how I regret my hasty action when I think I remember that so-and-so liked such-and-such's stock but, where once I had the information at my fingertips, it's no longer there. If you can find the space to store your catalogues, I strongly suggest that you do so.

At a benched show the number of your exhibit, and therefore your exhibit's bench number, will be marked on your pass, so, by now armed also with your catalogue, you can make your way to the bench, settle in your dog and organise your belongings and grooming equipment. Do try not to obstruct the bench next to your own for despite the fact that it may be empty when you arrive there is every chance that the exhibitor will turn up, and if she cannot get her dog on to her bench because it is already full of your coats and picnic hamper, you will have done nothing to find favour with your neighbour. Indeed, it is always helpful if you can strike up a friendly rapport with the person benched next to you because, being benched breed by breed in alphabetical order of surname, you will very often find yourself next to the same person and it can often be helpful to agree to keep an eye on each other's dogs from time to time.

For reasons of the safety of both exhibitors and their dogs, it is most important that gangways, passages and areas around rings are kept clear at shows. It is the responsibility of show societies to 'provide a place where dog boxes can be left' so if you have too much equipment to stack neatly under your bench, do please use the designated area.

# Benching your dog

When first you bench your dog it is sure to feel a little strange to him, so stay with him for a while so that he feels secure. When you feel he is confident enough for you to leave, stay within earshot just for a few moments at a time until you think it is safe to leave him for longer spells. Each time you return to his bench give him some warm words of praise and soon he will learn that as you always come back to him his bench is a good place to rest. Many dogs seem to adore their benches and it is surprising how they jump on and settle down as soon as they get to the show, just as if they have always had the very same old bench. There are, unfortunately, others who seem never to take to their bench and bark constantly, to the annoyance of every nearby exhibitor; fortunately, these are in the minority. If, however, your dog does turn out to be one of those incessant barkers, do stay with him on the bench for there is nothing worse than being benched next to a dog who sets up a great commotion every time his owner moves away. Some exhibitors do not leave their dogs unattended at any time and this is obviously the ideal where the safety of the dog is concerned. However, especially if travelling to a show alone, it is rarely possible to be with your dog all the time, so if you do have to leave the bench keep popping back to check on your dog at regular intervals and, if possible, ask a neighbour to keep a general eye on him. Always check that he is frequently offered a drink as well as the opportunity to relieve himself.

At a show which is unbenched, usually a show other than a General Championship show, you will keep your dog with you all the time. If you have a crate for your dog this can be very useful at such shows, but again, please be careful not to block gangways or fire exits. At some shows, especially Limited shows, the venues really are too small to take along all your equipment such as grooming tables, trolleys and crates, so to be fair to other exhibitors it is always a good idea to look over the hall to get your bearings before deciding how much of your equipment you should take inside.

## Ring numbers

At most benched shows you will find two copies of your dog's number on the bench; one number must always remain on the bench, while you will need to attach the other to your person with a ring-clip. If you don't already have a ring-clip (for they are rarely to be found in pet shops), don't panic; very many stall-holders sell them for about 25p each (unless you want to buy one of the more elaborate type depicting your breed). Bench numbers cannot be changed around, so don't swap your number with the empty bench next to you because it is better situated – you could easily find yourself in trouble for having done so. If there is only one copy of the number on your bench this will mean that numbers will be given out in the ring, so be sure to memorise your number because as you go into the ring you will have to ask the steward for it before setting up your dog; if you can't remember the number you will cause unnecessary delay while the steward looks up your dog's name in the catalogue and you will waste precious moments when you could have been preparing your dog for the judge's first glimpse of him.

At an unbenched show you may find that numbers are given out in the ring or you may have to collect them from the Secretary's table; because you will not have been sent a pass you will be reliant upon your catalogue for your number, but if you don't have a catalogue the Secretary will be able to look it up for you. Always make sure you have checked before your class is scheduled to go in the ring that you know from where you are to obtain your number; you do not want to find yourself in the embarrassing position of going into the ring numberless, only to find that you should have collected it from the Secretary or from your bench, in which case the judging will have to be held up while your number is obtained.

## Another piece of useful advice

Before closing this chapter, please don't take offence if I give you a little advice about going to the lavatory. You, I mean, not your dog. Of course, show societies try their best to provide adequate amenities but toilet facilities do vary from show to show. Although they often seem to be, it is in fact rare that the nearest loo is located at the other end of the field, but if you are really unlucky the portable cabin at your end of the showground could be in the process of being emptied, or may have run out of water, albeit temporarily. Such an inconvenience causes an extra long queue at the functioning facilities, and even at an indoor show you can be virtually certain that when you want to pay a visit the rest of the world does too.

As a result I would strongly advise you to plan ahead. If there is a service station or a public loo shortly before you get to the venue, use it. It's even worth popping a few pounds' worth of petrol in your tank or buying a packet of crisps at a suitable filling station if it has a loo you can use. Failing that, if you find upon arrival that there is a loo just inside the entrance to the showground (there sometimes is) and you have someone with you who can look after your dog for a moment, use it then; the queue is usually shorter at the beginning of the day. Always have a tissue in your pocket when you visit (paper often seems to have run out) and don't take your dog along to the loo with you – they are sometimes not allowed in, and if you have to use one of the portable varieties you will have quite enough trouble trying to manoeuvre yourself behind the door without the added encumbrance of your dog. Lastly and most importantly, allow yourself plenty of time. It is highly likely that you will have to walk a good distance, stand in a long queue or meet someone who wants to chat with you on the way there, so don't pay a visit just before your dog's class is due in the ring, or you may just miss it.

# 5

# Handling

As a handler you will be expected to know exactly what is required within your own breed, roughly at what speed it is acceptable to move your dog, and how to use the lead; in some breeds you will find that the lead is draped loosely around the neck while the dog is standing, whereas in others it can be held tightly. You must also know the correct stance for your breed and how the judge expects to see the tail. In many of the Gundog breeds the tail is held out by the handler, whereas in some other breeds it should be carried over the back or held erect. If your dog does not hold the tail correctly of his own accord, you will need

*The Irish Setter's tail is being held out by the exhibitor*

*Pekingese are shown differently from other breeds. They are all placed on the table head-on to the judge as seen here*

discreetly to hold it in position while the dog is stacked. You will also need to know whether your dog is stood in profile (usually head facing to the handler's right) or head-on to the judge, as for Pekingese and some of the Bull breeds. Similarly, you must know whether your dog is to be seen by the judge on the table (a 'table dog') or on the ground, or you may have a Yorkshire Terrier which, before it is put on the table for the judge's inspection, is shown standing on a show case.

In some breeds dogs are always shown with the exhibitor in a standing position, the owner using bait to attract the dog's attention, while for other breeds the handlers often kneel behind the dog and rarely use bait at all. If you have to kneel with your dog, try to keep your back fairly straight and don't get yourself

*When exhibiting one of the smaller breeds it is often necessary for the handler to stoop*

into such a position that you cannot rise again quickly when expected to do so; ladies should be careful not to catch the heel of their shoe in the hem of their skirt (check all hems before going to a show – sounds a bit pedantic but it is worth while).

As a good handler you will be conscious of your dog's temperament and whether he is likely to be put off by his environment in the ring. Remember that even the most soundly constructed dog can stand as if he is unsound if he is at all nervous or apprehensive: he might stand with his hocks turned in or might not put his forelegs in a correct line with his shoulder blades, or even, due to tension, spread his toes so that he appears to be splay-footed. As a good handler you will have practised with your dog on all types of floor surface so that he is not put off when he suddenly encounters a slippery floor or coloured lines drawn on the floor of an indoor venue at a leisure centre. If your dog does find it difficult to keep his grip on a slippery floor, it will help if you moisten his feet just slightly before he goes into the ring.

## Watching other exhibitors

Before the time comes for you to go into the ring with your dog, unless you are in the very first class for your breed or the first class being judged by this particular judge, you will have had an opportunity to watch exactly what the judge has expected of previous exhibitors. If you have watched carefully you will be better prepared when your own turn comes, for most judges keep to more or less the same sequence for each class. If you are at an outdoor show you should have observed any large pot-holes before going into the ring, for this will prevent you, and your dog, from walking straight through them and running the risk of tripping up or, at worst, going head over heels. Believe me, it has been done. By no means all outdoor rings have perfectly smooth and even surfaces.

## At the beginning of the class

Once in the ring, with your number pinned on by your ring-clip in a place which can be easily seen by steward, judge and preferably also the ring-side audience, take your place at the edge of the ring as indicated by the steward. You will usually find that the line of

*Miniature Dachshunds have to be weighed in at the beginning of each class before judging commences*

new dogs to be seen is to the right of the judge's table. If you have not shown before, avoid being first in the line so that you can have a few extra moments to get yourself together. If you can, try to avoid standing your dog next to the one which you feel sure is going to win, or the one that is in abundant coat when your own is still looking a little immature. Keep your eye on the judge from the moment you enter the ring and avoid ever allowing your dog to stand in an ungainly position, for the judge will often give the dogs a cursory glance while she sips her cup of coffee between classes. It is not necessary for your dog to stand in a show pose throughout the class because that can be too tiring, especially for a younger dog, and he is always likely to fidget if kept standing for too long. However, when he is relaxed, perhaps in a sitting posture, his head should ideally be facing the judge in case she happens to look his way between dogs; under no circumstances allow him to stand awkwardly, for example with his hind legs in a cow-hocked stance. You are in that ring to display your dog's attributes, not his weak points. Having said that, if you are in an outside ring on a very hot day and the judge is going over the other exhibits in the class, it is perfectly acceptable to position both yourself and your dog in such a fashion that your body provides him with some degree of shade.

A soundly constructed and well-behaved dog will often automatically stand in a correct show pose, but you may wish to put a finishing touch to his stance or improve upon the positioning of his legs to enhance a desirable feature, or conceal a not so desirable one. To get his front legs into position, lift the whole of the front assembly, supporting the lower section of the rib-cage (under the brisket and just behind the dog's elbow) with your left hand and, using your right hand to support the dog under the jaw, lower the front again; you should find that the feet are where you would like them to be if the dog has well-constructed forequarters. If, however, you still wish to make an adjustment (for whatever reason) you can lift each leg individually from just below the elbow, thus guiding the foot into the correct place. Before doing this you must see to it that the head of the dog is facing directly forwards for if not you could throw him off balance so that he ends up standing in a worse position than the one you were attempting to improve. The front feet should ideally fall directly below the centre of the shoulder blade. So often one sees dogs standing perfectly well, only to be lifted by their over-enthusiastic handlers and put down again looking somewhat like a rocking-horse. In breeds which are shown with the handler standing to attract the dog's attention, often the handler uses her foot to nudge the dog's foot gently into the desired position.

You will have noticed that the stance of the back legs differs considerably according to the breed. If you have watched carefully you will also possibly have noticed that if a dog is rather high on the back-end, the handler will often stretch out the back legs a little further than is natural for the dog. This has the effect of making the hindquarters drop a bit lower and the top-line consequently has the appearance of being more level than it actually is (such a manoeuvre rarely goes unnoticed by a good judge but it can sometimes be worth a try). Always make sure the fore legs are in the correct position before you attempt to move either of the back ones, then if you need to change the position of one of the legs, keeping your right hand near the dog's front, grasp the hind leg firmly but gently with your left hand and you will find that you can direct the foot into the required position. Never touch your dog's foot to move his position for in almost every case you will find that he simply moves it again as soon as you release your hand.

In the smaller breeds you will often find it possible to let the hind feet fall into the correct position by lifting the quarters from under the crutch and gently dropping them into position. With some breeds, especially those which are shown from the handler's standing position, it is found easier to move the dog around, usually in a small circle on the spot, before letting him find the correct position naturally. If you have a dog which tends to lean towards you (this can frequently happen if a dog is nervous), a little tap on the side of the ribs will often correct this.

In some cases, especially if you have a fidgety puppy, you may find that you need to hold him firmly under the chin to keep his head pointing in the right direction. If you need to support his head in this way, do try not to let four fingers spoil the view of the dog as seen by the judge. You should find that your hand can be almost completely concealed in the fold of skin under the lower jaw; nothing looks more unsightly than your fingers creeping up the show side of the muzzle.

As mentioned earlier, if you are involved in one of the Gundog breeds you may find that in your breed the dog's tail is to be extended outwards with your left hand in a line with the dog's back. Again it does tend to give a neater finished appearance if you can conceal your hand behind the flag of the tail. In the Terrier breeds it is often necessary to support the tail so that it is held in the desired position, or to stroke it lightly so that it falls at the correct tilt.

If yours is a breed in which titbits are used for baiting, do make sure that you hold the bait at the right height so that the dog holds his head at the correct angle, and don't let him eat large chunks of goodies in the ring. He will soon learn that he can have only the odd lick or a tiny piece and that he will be well rewarded when the judging is complete. Never bait a dog without giving him his justly deserved reward at the end.

It is perfectly acceptable to take a brush or comb into the ring with you if you wish, but do try not to leave it behind on the judging table or drop it out of your pocket as you move around the ring, for if you do you will most probably be worrying about where you last saw your comb rather than concentrating on your dog. Your brush or comb (note I suggest either one or the other, not both) need not be kept out of sight of the judge, but do try not to titivate too much while the judge is looking at your dog. It is only too easy to be concentrating on presenting every hair to perfection and, in doing so, masking the dog just as the judge is casting that all-important glance in his direction. On a particu-

*Titbits used for baiting must be held at the right height so that the dog holds its head at the correct angle*

larly windy day, if you have a long-coated breed you will have virtually no chance of getting every hair in the right place for more than a second or so, so you may as well let the wind take its toll in the knowledge that every other exhibit in the class is suffering in the same way. On the subject of wind, if your dog's coat is blowing back over his head because of a strong wind, thereby totally spoiling his outline and probably also his ability to see very much, you would be well advised to turn him round to face the opposite direction, which should look more aesthetically pleasing for the judge. Some dogs don't like to have the wind blowing up their nostrils, however, in which case you may indeed find it better to be facing the opposite direction. In any case, you can take some comfort from the fact that on especially windy days judges of long-coated breeds often ask to carry out their judging inside, although in this case there is every probability that you will have noisily flapping tents to contend with. When all is said and done, if you are showing a long-coated breed on a blustery day you will have a problem day ahead. But that's just one of the aspects which makes dog showing such fun!

Whatever the weather, if you happen to have landed yourself next to an over-chatty exhibitor it is best to politely turn a deaf ear and concentrate on your dog – after all, you have only a short while in the ring with your exhibit, so make the most of it. You could also be unlucky enough to end up next to a dog which is over-exuberant, one which insists on examining your own dog's rear quarters, or worse still one which seems to be on the ferocious side. Should such a misfortune befall you, make sure you keep as much distance as possible between your own dog and the less well-behaved one; if things get really out of hand the steward will probably intervene, but if not there is no harm at all in moving your dog to the back of the line so that it is the last exhibit to be seen by the judge. The fault is that of the other exhibitor who should keep his or her dog under better control. Don't think that this happens with any frequency, but it's better to know how to handle the situation should it occur.

# Moving the dogs together

Many judges like to move all the dogs round the ring together once or twice before they look at each dog individually. If you are first in the ring always listen for the judge's instructions as to how many circuits he would like you to make, for this may vary depending upon the class. For example, a judge may like to see the puppies move around the ring twice to give them time to settle but in the adult classes may ask them to go round only once. On the other hand, if the breed is a large one it may be necessary to move the dogs at least twice around the ring to get them into their stride, especially if the ring is not a large one. If a class of dogs is extremely large in number it may be necessary for the judge to divide the class into two and move first half the class and then the other half; this is more likely to happen in the large fast-gaited breeds, and occasionally, if space in the ring is very restricted, the judge may ask half the exhibits to wait outside the ring, thereby judging half the class at a time. Having said all that, some judges don't bother to move the dogs together at all, and at some of the smaller Sanction, Limited and Open shows there is simply not the space to do so.

If you are asked to move your dog around with the rest at the beginning of a class, leave yourself a good gap behind the dog in front so that your own dog's movement is not restricted in any way. If, as sometimes happens, the dog in front of yours 'plays up', deciding not to walk or even to do his business in the ring (yes, he should have been allowed to do this before but accidents can, and do, happen), don't wait too long but move your dog past him, always round the outside so that you cannot be accused of obstructing the judge's view of the other exhibit. When the dogs have finished moving there is no need for you to end up in your original position, but if the other exhibitor wishes to bring her dog back in front of yours it is best to let her do so. If, as you move round the ring, you need to adjust the lead because it is caught, for example, under the chin, do this quickly while you and your exhibit are at the rear of the judge so that your dog looks just right as you go through her line of vision. Don't under any circumstances have yards of lead dangling down; it should all be tidily wound up in your hand so that it does not detract from the dog. Indeed, a dangling lead can be most distracting for a judge and is a sure sign of a novice or careless exhibitor, so try to remember to avoid this if you can.

Another thing that needs attention (before you go into the ring, of course) is that if you have your dog on a choke chain it is on the right way round. The chain must be looped so that it will release easily when you pull to bring the dog to attention; put the chain on the wrong way and the choke will not release at all, making life uncomfortable for the dog and meaning that all your efforts at correction will be in vain. Assuming that you will be showing your dog on your left-hand side, the easiest way to be sure of having the chain correct is to try it out on your own left wrist. If the loop through which the chain slides is pointing upwards (nearest the thumb), you will see that as you jerk it with your right hand it automatically releases; if the loop is pointing downwards, when you jerk the chain it will hold fast.

The type of lead, or collar and lead combination, that you use will very much depend upon the breed you are showing. A Staffordshire Bull Terrier, for example, would look rather foolish in a delicate gold-coloured slip lead, and it would also be most impractical, for you could not restrain such a strong animal on that type of lead. On the other hand, it would look just as incongruous to see a little Yorkshire Terrier in a thick leather collar. However, in many of the larger breeds a 'show lead' is used in the ring, but outside the ring a much more sturdy collar is worn because this is more sensible when walking around the show-ground and, at a benched show, can be attached to the benching chain. Never think of trying to attach a benching chain to a choke chain or to a slip lead or your dog could very easily come to grief, if he doesn't escape first.

If your breed is one which has a long coat or a dense mane you will have to select your lead very carefully as you will not want one which will pull out too much coat. Apart from using trial and error you will almost certainly find that other exhibitors will help to guide you as to what sort of lead you should buy, but it has to be said that virtually everyone has their own personal preference. Don't ever select a lead which is far too long, for a long lead serves no useful purpose in the ring; it will simply mean that you have an extra foot or so to conceal in the palm of your hand or to wind around your arm.

## Individual assessment

The judge will now bring each dog out to judge separately. Depending primarily upon the size of the breed, your dog will be judged either on the table or on the floor. If the latter, you should stand your dog in the position indicated by the judge; if on the table, there will usually be a rubber mat indicating where you should stand the dog, but always remember that the judge has to

*If you have a large breed the judge will go over your dog on the ground*

be able to get at the dog so don't stand him in such a position that the judge has to lean over several feet of table before she can get her hands on him. If you do, you will most probably be asked to stack him again in the intended position. Also remember that however well-behaved your dog you must have control of him at all times and thus it is incorrect to drop the lead so that you release the dog entirely – indeed, to do so would be to break Kennel Club rules. You will, however, still want to conceal any surplus part of the lead and if your dog is now standing on a table you will have another couple of feet or so of lead to contend with. This may be looped around the back of your own neck so that you have both hands free to deal with your dog, or, as is favoured by many, just roll up the lead in one hand so that only a very short amount of it is showing above the dog's neck. Do be careful, though, that the lead does not impede the judge as she goes over your dog.

Most judges like to stand back to take a good look at the dog in profile before they approach him, usually from the front, so don't stand your dog facing in the wrong direction so that the judge has to peer round the award board to get a good view. If you do this you will very probably be asked to turn him round and it is likely that you will have begun to infuriate the judge, which will not improve your chances of winning. Most good judges approach first with their hand and a word of greeting, so as not to take the dog by surprise. If you are at all unsure about the temperament of your dog, be sure that you hold him firmly so that you can restrict him if he tries to back away, or indeed if you think he is likely to smother the judge in kisses. If your dog snaps at the judge or shows any sign of viciousness, you may be asked to withdraw him from the class, something the judge is well within her rights to request, and if this is the case you must seriously consider whether or not you should pursue a show career for the dog concerned. Viciousness in the show-ring is not to be tolerated, and it goes without saying that it would also be unwise to use a temperamentally unsound dog for breeding purposes.

A slight nervousness of the dog, without any sign of him snapping, is quite another matter and will need very careful handling of the situation on your part. The most common reaction of a nervous dog is to back away from the judge, so that he either virtually sits on his haunches or leans on you, the exhibitor. You will need to be firm and not to give in to the dog's fear; he must feel your confidence coming through. If he tends to back off, be sure to keep one hand firmly on his rear quarters to prevent him from drawing backwards; if he tends to lean on you, your spare hand will need to be towards the back of his rib-cage or on his coupling in an effort to keep him standing firmly. Don't be afraid to give him encouragement, talking to him all the while, and it also helps if you, his owner, can be in his line of vision so that he is sure you are there. Never forget to support that head, firmly under the chin, so that you are quite certain that he cannot rear up in fear and catch the judge, albeit unwittingly. Occasionally you can find that a bitch will show perfectly happily most of the time but shows an element of uneasiness shortly before her season and while she is in season. In such a case use your own judgement as to whether she should be shown at that time. I do not agree with in-season bitches being shown for I think it unfair on the male dogs which are being exhibited, but technically there is nothing to stop you from doing so. Nevertheless, even if you

*Different breeds are shown in different ways. This Staffordshire Bull Terrier is shown head-on, whilst his handler keeps a careful eye on the judge*

have paid your entry fees it may be wiser to let a slightly nervous bitch get over her season before you put her back in the ring. If you find that she regularly has a distinct change of temperament which makes her difficult to handle around the time of her season, you might be well advised to consult someone who specialises in homoeopathic medicine in an endeavour to sort out what is most probably a slight hormone imbalance.

Under normal circumstances you will, by now, be standing your dog in the position required for the breed. You should have practised at home, either in front of a mirror or with the aid of a friend, so that you know your dog looks as good as he possibly can. It is usual to move your dog into the position where the judge will go over him while the preceding dog is moving; this gives you a moment to stack your dog to advantage and saves the judge having to wait while you set up your dog. In setting up, though, under no circumstances must you restrict the judge's view of the other exhibit, so always walk behind the judge, never in front of her. Most judges ask the age of the dog in the age classes (i.e. Minor Puppy, Puppy, Junior, Special Yearling and Veteran) and many ask the age in all classes, although strictly speaking it is not necessary in those classes which are not restricted by age, for the judge is selecting the dogs on their merits, not on merits in accordance with age. However, do be sure that you know your dog's age whatever class you are in, for some judges feel that only by asking the age can they make a fair assessment in every respect. For example, an over-mature youngster may be entered in a class with dogs much older than he because he would otherwise stand out as being too large in stature in the puppy class. On the other hand, a judge might find by asking the age that a dog is, in reality, fully mature while it still looks only a youngster, most probably indicating that it has not developed the substance expected of the breed in maturity. Another reason for a judge asking a dog's age can simply be as an aid to get dog and exhibitor to relax. Obviously a judge cannot and should not enter into deep conversation with each exhibitor, but to go over a dog in complete silence makes for a somewhat stiff approach and a simple question about age breaks down that barrier. The judge will usually begin by going over the dog's head, measuring the skull proportions, the set and possibly the length of the ear, inspecting the size, shape, placement and colour of the eye, the pigment, the shape of the jaw and the positioning and possibly also the number of teeth. Exactly what the judge checks depends to a certain extent on the breed in question; in a few breeds, the Pekingese for example, it is frowned upon if a judge looks in the mouth of the dog, whereas in other breeds even the number of molars and pre-molars are frequently checked. The majority of judges open the dog's mouth themselves but others will ask you to do it for them. Don't be confused by the fact that some will ask to see the dog's teeth while others will refer to the mouth or the bite;

just keep in mind that the judge has no desire to inspect the back of your animal's throat but wishes primarily to see the placement of the teeth. In many breeds the judge will be interested only in seeing the bite but in others she will wish to check for missing teeth, see the condition of the teeth and perhaps the pigment on the lips and gums. Holding the lower jaw with your right hand, lower the bottom lip and, with your left hand placed across the muzzle, you will be able to raise the upper lips away from the teeth with your thumb on one side and fingers on the other. Some exhibitors like to show the dog's teeth themselves, especially if their dog is on the nervous side or is still teething. If you prefer to show your dog's bite yourself, even under a judge who is opening the mouths, it is common courtesy to ask politely if you may do so. It is usually at this point, or as she approaches the dog, that the judge will ask the dog's age, so make sure you know before you go into the ring so that you don't have to think about it for too long, furtively counting up the months on your fingers.

Usually the judge will then examine the dog's forequarters, neck and shoulders before going over the body, then will check tail set, length of tail in some breeds and the hindquarters. It is

*Here the exhibitor is showing her Deerhound's teeth so that the judge can see the bite*

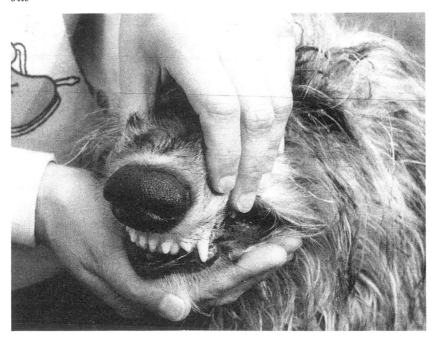

possible that the feet may be lifted by the judge for inspection; frequently this is to assess not only the size and shape of the foot but also the thickness of the pads. In male dogs the judge will, of course, also check to see that the dog has two testicles fully descended into the scrotum. In most cases both testicles will have descended before the dog is old enough to enter a show but occasionally, even though there may be two, a youngster can retract one due to tension or sometimes cold. If you are unfortunate enough to have a puppy which tends to retract a testicle now and again, hang on to them while you are in the ring. This is not as stupid as it sounds and can, you will find, be done quite discreetly so that no one has any idea of the strange things that are going on, especially if your dog has a reasonable coat (luckily the only dog for which I had to do this was an Afghan, so no one was any the wiser). The warmth of your hand will keep the testicle descended, and if all goes well, as your dog matures he will grow out of this unfortunate habit. On the subject of testicles (you will find that show people talk quite openly about the various private parts of their dogs' anatomy), it is technically possible to show a dog without two testicles, but most judges will penalise this very heavily for every Kennel Club Breed Standard states that two should be fully descended. If a testicle has had to be removed for surgical reasons it is possible to carry with you a veterinary statement to that effect, but a castrated dog cannot be shown unless he has already sired progeny which have been registered with the Kennel Club.

## Moving your dog individually

When the judge has gone over your dog she will ask you to move him, and by this stage you should have had the chance of watching to see how the other dogs have moved. Nothing will show you up as a novice more than setting off round the ring in the opposite direction to that indicated. It is for the judge to stipulate how she wants you to move; the triangle is favoured by many, but there are various other patterns in which you may be asked to move.

Before you begin to move your dog, whatever the pattern required, remember that the way you start off is absolutely vital, so don't rush or feel embarrassed that you are keeping the judge waiting. Firstly, remember not to block the judge's view of the exhibit, even at this early stage in the proceedings. If you have a table dog you can move round the back of the judge to get to your position if necessary, but if your dog is one which is gone over on the floor you may need to do a quick lead change so that you do not cross the judge's path. Take your time and set up your dog facing away from the judge in the direction in which he is to move; if you like, look up quickly and find a 'marker' at which you feel you should aim and then, as you turn, take a quick glance at the judge to see that you are heading off again in the right direction.

# The triangle

If asked to do a triangle do just that, not an arc nor a square; by asking you to move in a triangle what the judge is hoping to see is a clear view of the hind movement as you move away, the dog in profile as you go across the top of the triangle and the dog's front movement as you come back towards her. If a judge has indicated a large triangle don't cut the top end short, for, given that the ring is of adequate size, that is where the judge will be assessing the profile of the dog in action. A correctly executed triangle allows the judge to see every aspect of a dog's movement in the shortest possible time and has the advantage that the judge can remain more or less stationary in the corner of the ring. It sounds simple enough, but you would be surprised how many people seem quite incapable of moving their dog in a triangle when asked to do so, so I would strongly suggest that you study these simple diagrams and practise before you make your first entry into the ring with your new show dog.

*Figure 2*

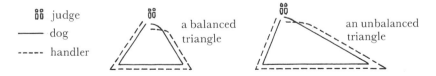

judge
—— dog
----- handler

a balanced triangle

an unbalanced triangle

# The 'L' and the 'T'

The 'L' or reverse 'L' is a pattern which is sometimes used in a small indoor venue where the dogs need to move on mats, so in many cases you will have the benefit of rubber matting to help keep you in the desired direction. By the way, if you go to a show where there is matting the idea is that either both you and the dog move on the matting or, if it is less wide, that the dog moves on the matting and you move on the floor. Please don't walk proudly along the matting yourself, leaving your dog to slither and slide along a slippery floor!

The 'L' shape has the advantage for the judge that he can see both sides of the dog moving, but the disadvantage for you is that you will have to change the lead into the other hand when you get to the end of the 'L'. Were you not to do so (so that the dog goes back to the judge moving on your right) you would come between your dog and the judge, thereby masking his view.

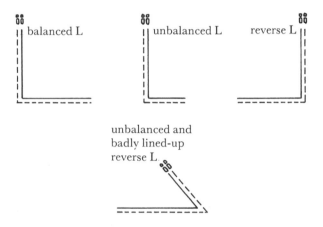

*Figure 3*

The 'T' shape is rarely used in the ring but it is important to know of its existence for it can be used in Junior Handling competitions, for example. This pattern is somewhat complex as it involves two lead changes but is quite a useful exercise to practise so that you can cope with any eventuality.

*Figure 4*

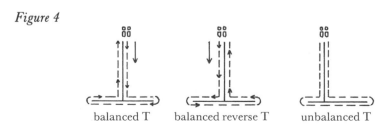

# Moving up and down

In addition to the triangle or perhaps the 'L', many judges also ask you to move once up and down or perhaps diagonally across the ring, so that they can have yet another look at the dog's movement fore and aft. Whatever you do (and remember that it is acceptable to avoid pot-holes and, for that matter, tent poles), this is a time to remember once again that you must never come between your dog and the judge's view of him. This means that if asked to move 'up and down' as you turn you must go round the back of your dog and not allow the dog to go round you. Remember to apply this rule at all times; it is most important.

*Figure 5*

Often in an indoor venue where space is limited the rings are not big enough to have anything more than one mat up and down the centre of the ring. In this case the judge will often ask you to move twice. Usually she will start by watching your dog from the end of the mat and will then, on the second occasion, move to the side so that she can see him in profile. Again remember the golden rule: don't come between the judge and your dog. This means that as you get to the top of the mat you will need to change the lead to your other hand so that your dog moves down the mat again in complete view of the judge.

As already mentioned, it is up to the judge to decide where you move and some judges ask slightly different things of different breeds, or according to the size and shape of the ring or the number of dogs in a class. Another possibility is that you may be asked to move in a triangle and then take your dog back to the end of the line, possibly via a wide arc. In this case make sure that you are still concentrating on your dog's movement, for the judge will most probably still be looking at him as you move back to your place. Indeed, whenever you are moving your dog in the ring, even if not specifically for the judge, make sure that your dog is moving as well as possible because the judge may just be giving him a second glance even though you are not aware of it.

So you have moved your dog at the pace you feel is correct for him, something you will have practised ideally with the aid of a friend who will have been able to tell you whether he is moving in as true a line as possible. When you have found the right pace, keep to it on all occasions and alter that pace only if the judge asks you specifically to do so. All the while you should keep in mind that the judge will be looking for different aspects of the dog's movement, depending upon the direction in which the dog is travelling. As he moves away the judge will be assessing whether the hind legs are the correct distance apart or whether they are too close, too wide or are displaying a certain weakness such as cow hocks. She will also be looking to see whether the dog is showing the correct amount of pad for its breed, as well as judging drive from behind. As she watches in profile she will be looking for carriage of head, top-line and tail, general balance and length of the front and back strides and how well they complement one another. For example, a dog which has great extension in the hind quarters but a more limited front stride (usually because it is upright in shoulder or short in upper arm) will over-reach, a fault which can be seen very clearly in profile. When moving towards the judge she will be looking to see how the fore-legs are moving, whether the dog is loose or too tight in elbow, and checking for faults in the pasterns or feet. A clever handler can sometimes hide a fault while the dog is stacked, but a good judge will usually spot it when he is on the move, so you really must be sure that you are moving your dog to its best advantage at all times in order to make the most of his virtues and minimise his faults.

When you have moved you will usually (Yorkshire Terriers are an exception) take your place at the back of the line while the judge goes over the next exhibit, so that by the time the judge has finished seeing all the dogs you will all be back where you started, or at least in the same order. Just a word of warning here: if you are in an indoor venue where dogs are expected to move on the mats provided, do be careful not to obstruct the mat while other exhibits are moving for the judge. This so often happens – everyone shuffles along in line and some seem oblivious of the fact that they are actually standing on the very mat which is being used as part of the triangle. In such an event, just move your dog to one side for a moment until the path is clear and you can then move into a position in the line but not obstructing the mat. If your dog is small enough you may hold him in your arms if you wish; this is often the easiest way of keeping him where you want him when in a tight corner.

# The final assessment

Sooner or later the judge will have finished seeing each dog individually and will then very probably walk up and down the line to take a look at all the dogs standing together. If at all possible, try at this stage to have your dog standing on a level piece of ground. If the ground slopes steeply downwards in front of you your dog may look high on the back-end even though he is not. Sometimes it is impossible to avoid such a slope and if you feel it necessary you may turn your dog to face in the opposite direction. There are, however, varying opinions as to whether dogs should be allowed to face 'the other way round', for undoubtedly it does not allow the judge to have a frontal view of all the exhibits at once. I would suggest that you change the direction of your dog only if you have good reason to do so, such as a steep slope or a very strong wind which, if you are showing a long-coated dog, is causing the coat to blow over the head and eyes. There can, though, be other good reasons for turning your dog in another direction. If you have a dog with a light eye you would be well advised to avoid letting him face the sun or a strong light for that will make the eye look even lighter; if you have a mis-marked dog, or one with an unusual marking or coat pattern which is likely to give a less appealing picture to the judge, that would be another good reason for at least trying to get away with standing your dog in the opposite direction, although the judge might always ask you to turn back again. Naturally, if you yourself have a handicap which prevents you from showing in the conventional manner, the judge will usually be most understanding.

While I have stressed that you should keep your eye on the judge at all times, this is the time at which you must pay particular attention to every signal that may be made. What the judge does next will depend on many things – the judge's own specific way of judging, the size of the class (which will have a bearing on whether the judge needs to refresh her memory about certain points on individual dogs) and the overall quality or lack of quality in the class. Very often a judge will now go to individual dogs to check certain points and may ask some to move again. In the latter case the judge will not usually expect you to take your dog in a full triangle again but will just ask you to move him a short way across the ring and back. Not all judges check points again in this manner but many do, especially breed specialists. Now is the time when the judge will call certain dogs into the centre of the ring, either for further consideration or for the final placings. In a large class you will often find that the judge pulls out about eight or ten, whereas in a smaller class she may pull out the exact number for which there will be awards – usually between four and six depending upon the show. Keep showing your dog to his full advantage right up to the point at which the judge dismisses the remainder, for she may pull out a few and then go back to the beginning of the line to select one or two more. Only when you know you have been dismissed should you relax your dog and lead him calmly out of the ring (without passing loud or unkind comment as to why your dog has been thrown out and someone else's has remained in the ring).

Of course, you may be one of those retained, but remember that the class is by no means over yet. It is possible that the judge will actually place the dogs as they are pulled out, but even then you must not stop showing your dog for she may still change her mind at the very last minute and swap two or more of them about. Added to this the judge will most probably want to take notes on her first prize-winners, and at Championship level and breed club Open shows she will also be required to take notes on the winner of the second prize. On the other hand, she may still wish to re-assess the dogs she has retained before deciding upon the final placings, in which case you will usually be asked to move back again to the edge of the ring while she makes a final assessment and perhaps checks a few more individual points. In this event she may well decide that she wishes to see these few dogs move again, either all together in a lap round the ring, or perhaps individually. In some cases, usually where there is a close decision between two dogs, a judge will ask that two exhibits be moved together. If this happens, ideally the judge will want to see the dogs side by side so you may have to move your dog on the opposite side to normal; however, if you think your dog will be put off by this, just move him as usual. The last thing you want to do is throw away your chances at this crucial moment.

# Final placings

When the judge seems to have decided on her final placings she will call the chosen dogs to the centre of the ring so that they are lined up from left to right. The steward will probably indicate where the dogs are to stand, but if you have watched the preceding classes carefully you should already have taken note of this in case you are one of the lucky ones. Unfortunately there are just a few exhibitors who always seem to manage (by design) to stand their dogs at the front of the line even though they have been called out to a lower place, possibly even VHC. Please don't be one of those exhibitors or you will make yourself very unpopular, for you can be sure that at least someone at the ring-side will have noticed your devious tactics. Actually such a move very rarely works because most judges (though admittedly not all) cast a last eye over their winners before instructing the steward to mark down the awards. The exhibitor who has jumped up a place or two is usually moved back to the place originally intended, often to the accompaniment of a knowing mutter from observers at the ring-side. On the very odd occasion that someone does get away with it – and it has to be said that this can happen from time to time – there surely can be no satisfaction for the exhibitor in having won in such an underhanded way. On the assumption that you are not the offending party, do be on your guard against such awkward exhibitors. If you know that you were called, shall we say, into second place and, like magic, someone has leapt into the spot before you get there, don't be afraid to say politely that you thought the judge intended that you should be there. Without causing a great incident, this should be enough to bring the judge's attention to what has happened and she will probably indicate exactly where each of you should stand. If you go briskly to your designated place you will lessen the chances of someone getting into 'your' spot before you.

And so the dogs in the class have finally been placed in order of the judge's choice, and with any luck your own dog is among them. Don't immediately rush out of the ring, but wait until the prize cards and (if you are lucky) rosettes and/or prize money (the latter sometimes stapled to the back of the prize card) have been presented and the numbers of the winners announced to the ring-side by the steward. Usually it is again the steward who hands out the awards while the judge marks up her judging book

*Yorkshire Terriers are exhibited on a show case. Here they have been placed by the judge and the ring steward is handing out prize cards and rosettes*

and makes notes. Then, and only then, you may leave the ring. However, it is usually considered courteous to give a brief word of congratulation to the winner before you leave the ring; this is especially so for the second and third prize-winners, just to show that although your dog has been beaten there are no hard feelings. You may or may not agree with the judge's selection but that is her prerogative and it is always considered good manners to be pleased for the winner of the class.

If your dog has been placed first, clearly you will be delighted. Do thank the judge for the honour but don't go overboard – there is no need to fling your arms round the judge or throw your hat high in the air. However pleased you are, do try to keep control. After you have left the ring be delighted about your win by all means, but don't boast about it. Always keep in the back of your mind that those to whom you are bragging may not have been placed themselves or may be strong supporters of one of the unplaced dogs. Similarly, if you are unplaced, whatever your private opinions about the prize-winners – or any other exhibits for that matter – you will be wiser to keep your comments to yourself.

If you have won a rosette you may, of course, display this on your person, on the dog's bench or crate or even on your handbag if you like; what you must not do is go into the show-ring on another occasion wearing a rosette that you have won. There are certain exceptions, such as if you have won a rosette for Best of Breed, which may be worn in the challenge for Best in Group or Best in Show.

## Competition in a subsequent class

When you made your entry for the show you may have decided to enter your dog in more than one class – Puppy and Novice, for example. Provided that the judge is the same for these two classes, you will, in your second and subsequent classes, become a 'seen dog', that is to say your dog has already been seen by this judge. If the judge is a different one, as may happen if you have entered one breed class and one Any Variety class, yours will be a 'new dog' and will be judged in the same way as outlined above. But let us go back to seen dogs for a moment. These will be lined up at the perimeter of the ring, usually on a different side from the new dogs which the judge has not yet assessed. It is the steward's job to line up these dogs in the order in which the judge has already placed them, but you would do well to have your own wits about you and note which other seen dogs have been placed, for mistakes can, and do, happen. The judge has every right to change the placings around if she wishes in a subsequent class, and this, indeed, is sometimes done, but I often have a sneaking suspicion that the placings have been altered in error rather than by judgement. In any event, the steward should place the dogs in order of their previous placing and will explain this order to the judge; if he is confronted with more than one prize-winner from previous classes he will usually group together the winners from each class. Naturally, just because a dog has won a first in one class does not automatically mean that the judge likes him better than the one she has placed second in another. Frequently a dog placed second in a Junior class has a very good chance of beating a first prize-winner in a Minor Puppy class, for example. If a judge is undecided between two exhibits she may well ask, 'Have you met?' In doing so, she is asking not if you are familiar with the other exhibitor indicated (it is honestly quite surprising how many novice exhibitors misinterpret this question) but whether your dogs have been shown in the same class as one another. A judge may be asking the question just to clarify things in her own mind, for unfortunately some stewards do make errors when lining up seen dogs and an unintentional reversal of placings can reflect badly on a judge.

When the judge has assessed all the new dogs the seen dogs, or 'old dogs' as they are often called, will usually be asked to move along to the end of the line so that the judge has a complete line-up of exhibits in that particular class. The judge may decide to move the seen dogs again and may go over some individual points, but rarely will she give another full examination. Indeed, she is not under any obligation even to touch these dogs again and may well not do so unless she is interested in placing them. There is, of course, nothing to prevent a good 'seen' dog winning a class over and above the 'new' exhibits, and in fact this often happens. However, do bear in mind when initially filling in your entry form that if your dog wins a first place in one class and is subsequently beaten in another, he will not be eligible to challenge for Best of Sex or Breed, as appropriate. This bears out the earlier suggestion that it is not wise to enter too many classes, nor to enter those in which the competition is likely to be too stiff for your dog. A dog which has a fair chance of winning a Novice class would probably be completely out of his depth in a Limit class, so if you have entered and won Novice, it would be a pity to ruin your chances of being seen in the line-up by also entering and subsequently being unplaced in Limit.

# Best of Breed

Provided that there is more than one class scheduled for your breed at a show, the winners of each class will, when the class judging for the breed is complete, be called into the ring to compete for Best of Sex or Best of Breed. In actual fact the judge is at liberty to call in only those dogs which she wishes to consider again, even if it is only one dog, but in practice it is usual for all unbeaten exhibits to line up for the judge. This, especially at a large show where there have been several classes scheduled, is always interesting for the ring-side audience.

Treat this just like a class. The judge will rarely wish to give another thorough examination of each dog but it is not unusual for each one to be moved again individually and for the judge to check certain features again. If undecided between two exhibits she may ask to look at them again together, possibly moving their places in the line-up so that they are standing next to one another.

Depending on the awards allocated at the show a Reserve Best of Sex or Reserve Best of Breed may also be declared, in which case the judge may, if she wishes, call into the ring for consideration the dog which has been placed second to that which she has declared Best of Breed or Best of Sex. If you have won a second in a class it is therefore very wise to remain near the ring-side with your dog, just in case you are called in again; it would be a pity to miss the opportunity because you had wandered off around the trade stands at the crucial moment. In many breeds it used to be common practice for the second prize-winner in the Open class to go into the ring with the class winners, but strictly speaking the owner of that dog has absolutely no right to join the line-up in this manner unless invited to do so after Best of Sex or Best of Breed has been awarded to the winner of the Open class.

At a show where Best of each sex is declared, the two winners are later assessed together and Best of Breed is decided between them. If a Reserve Best of Breed is also to be awarded, this does not necessarily have to go to the dog declared Best of the opposite sex but may be awarded to what the judge considers to be the second best of the same sex. I know that this all sounds highly complicated when put down on paper, but in reality it is not as complex as it appears, and in any event, as an exhibitor you will not be involved with the machinations of the awards. Provided that you are available so that you may go straight into the ring

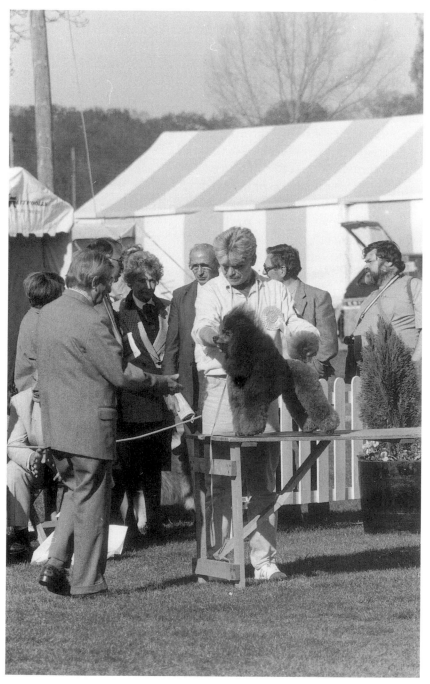

*This table dog has already won Best of Breed and is now about to be examined by the Group Judge. Note how the judge approaches with his hand extended*

with your dog if requested to do so, that is all you need to worry about. If you have won a first prize with your exhibit (and if it has not been beaten by another dog under the same judge), you should listen for the steward to make the usual cry of 'All unbeaten dogs [or bitches] please'. If you have won a second prize and the dog which beat your own is awarded Best of anything, be sure that you are visible so that the steward can find you if the judge wants you to take your dog into the ring to challenge for the Reserve spot.

# The Referee

At shows where there is one judge for dogs and another for bitches, the show society will also have had to appoint a Referee. The challenge for Best of Breed (or Best in Show at a single breed club show) will be between the Best of the dogs and the Best of the bitches and is decided upon jointly by the two judges. Naturally, their opinions may differ as to which is the better of the two, in which case the decision rests with the Referee. At breed club shows there can also be special awards for Best Junior, Best Post Graduate and so on; as for Best in Show, the decision is made jointly and the Referee is called in if the need arises. It is not unknown, however, for the judges to agree on all the final decisions so that the Referee is not called upon at all.

6

# Titles, prestigious awards and the judges themselves

To be highly placed in a class inevitably provides pleasure, and to go Best of Breed at Open show level gives yet another thrill, especially if your dog has overcome stiff competition to achieve this. But there are other awards and achievements which are not always immediately apparent to ring-siders and some of them take a little understanding to appreciate fully. I think most seasoned exhibitors will agree that the greatest thrill comes with one's very first 'CC'.

## Challenge Certificates

Challenge Certificates, commonly referred to as CCs, are awarded only at Championship shows and it is by winning these very special and highly elusive awards that a dog becomes a Champion. Challenge Certificates are granted by the Kennel Club and are not available for all breeds at all Championship shows, so do be careful to read show schedules carefully, especially if yours is one of the less popular breeds for which CCs are not always on offer. Usually, if there are no CCs on offer for a particular breed at a Championship show the entry fees are a little less than for other breeds, but it still costs more to enter than an Open show because the expense involved in running a Championship show is greater. We shall come to Cruft's qualifiers in a moment, but do also take into consideration that a dog cannot qualify for Cruft's unless CCs are on offer for the breed.

*Each of these two Shih Tzu has been awarded a Challenge Certificate following competition against its own sex at a Breed Club Championship Show. They are pictured here with the judge after Best in Show has been declared*

A Challenge Certificate is undeniably a very high accolade, because even if a dog wins only one of these in its lifetime it means that a judge is prepared to sign a document to say that she feels the dog is worthy of being a Champion. When on offer, one Kennel Club Challenge Certificate is made available for the Best of each sex, and it is, of course, only unbeaten dogs which can challenge for this award. The wording on a Challenge Certificate is: 'I am clearly of the opinion that . . . owned by . . . is of such outstanding merit as to be awarded the title of Champion.'

*Figure 6*

*Figure 7*

The wording is clear, and if the judge does not feel that any of the exhibits are of high enough standard to be awarded a Certificate then the CC may be withheld. Invariably, if a judge does withhold there is a sense of intense unease among the exhibitors and clearly it takes a certain strength of character on the part of the judge, for by the act of withholding she is effectively stating that not one of the dogs entered is worthy of the title of Champion. This must be particularly difficult for a judge if there are several exhibits in the ring which already carry such a title, and naturally, exhibitors are likely to be upset about such a decision. However, judges who accept Championship show appointments must, of necessity, have the courage of their own convictions and it would be wrong of them to award a CC if they did not feel that one of the exhibits was worthy of receiving it. It is, of course, possible for a judge to award the CC for one sex and not for the other. Naturally, if the Challenge Certificate is withheld then the Reserve Challenge Certificate must be withheld also.

Fortunately, witholding is the exception rather than the rule for at most Championship shows there are some top-quality dogs entered in each breed. Indeed, quite often one reads reports of judges having said that they wish they had had more than one Certificate to hand out. Upon winning a CC a green and white card, duly completed and signed by the judge, is given to the exhibitor in the ring and the Kennel Club then posts the actual Certificate to the exhibitor's home a short while afterwards.

## Reserve Challenge Certificate

When CCs are available there is also a Reserve Challenge Certificate on offer for each sex. Although Reserve CCs do not count towards the title of Champion, in awarding the Certificate the judge is again effectively stating that a dog or bitch is worthy of the title of Champion, for if the winner of the CC is disqualified for some reason (it happens very rarely but has been known) then the winner of the Reserve CC is awarded the CC instead. A Reserve Challenge Certificate actually states: 'I am clearly of the opinion that . . . owned by . . . is of such outstanding merit as to be awarded the Challenge Certificate should the Challenge Certificate winner be disqualified.'

Thus, once again the judge may withhold if she sees fit, and naturally, if the Challenge Certificate is withheld the Reserve

THREE COUNTIES *Championship Show* *Date* 14TH JUNE 1

*Breed* LHASA APSOS *Sex* BITCH

## Kennel Club
## Reserve
## Challenge Certificate

*I am clearly of the opinion that*
Tabbic Tu of Jontors
*(Name of Exhibit)*
*owned by* Misses J.P.A. Cunliffe & C.A. Johnson
*(Name of Owner)*
*is of such outstanding merit as to be worthy of being*
*awarded the Challenge Certificate should the Challenge*
*Certificate winner be disqualified.*

*(Signed)* S. Chandler *(Judge)*

*Figure 8*

Certificate must not be issued either. Winners of a Reserve CC are given a slightly smaller green and white card in the ring and this, like the CC, is signed by the judge.

Reserve CCs are certainly something of which one can be very proud. It is an honour to win a Reserve CC, but it can also be infuriating if one's dog manages to get two CCs and ten or more Reserves, thus never attaining the title of Champion, and one can certainly sympathise with those whose dogs never quite make it.

## The title of Champion

A Champion is a dog which has won three Challenge Certificates under three different judges, at least one of which must have been awarded after the dog was twelve months of age. There are, however, a few exceptions to complicate the issue. In the case of Border Collies and dogs within the Gundog group, three CCs give them the title of Show Champion (Sh. Ch.) for they need also to

# THE KENNEL CLUB

This is to certify that
Misses J. P. Cunliffe & C. A. Johnson's Lhasa Apso
TABBI TU OF JONTERS

has qualified for the title of

## CHAMPION

under Kennel Club Rules and Regulations

10th August, 1984

Signed

*Executive Officer*

1 Clarges Street
PICCADILLY
LONDON W1Y 8AB

*Figure 9*

hold further qualifications if they are to lay claim to the full title of Champion. In Chapter 10 you will find the Kennel Club's ruling in this regard.

The owner of a dog which has qualified as a Champion will automatically be forwarded a certificate from the Kennel Club and has the right to use the title of Champion (usually seen as Ch.) in front of the dog's name at any time. The Kennel Club also forwards a Breeder's Certificate to the breeder of the Champion – a rather nice touch, as all too frequently if the successful dog is not bred by its owner the actual breeder tends to be overlooked.

Many people quite naturally wish to advertise the fact that their dog has become a Champion immediately after the big day occurs. In such cases when, inevitably, the official confirmation has not channelled its way through the Kennel Club, advertisements should carry the note 'Subject to KC confirmation' after the name of the dog. The names of all Champions are published in the *Kennel Gazette* and notification can also be found in the KC Stud Book and Breed Record Supplements.

# Best in Group and Best in Show

At any type of show in which breed classes are scheduled, the dogs declared Best of Breed will be eligible to compete either for Best in Group or Best in Show. Many of the smaller shows do not judge on a group system, in which case the Best of Breed winners go straight through to compete for Best in Show. At General Championship shows and some of the larger Open shows all the best of Breed winners meet the other winners within their own group and a Group Winner and Reserve Group Winner are declared. The Winner then goes on to compete against the winners of all the other five groups so that one of them may be declared Best in Show. A Reserve Best in Show is also declared.

Once again this is quite straightforward in practice, but in the case of a show which spans more than one day it does mean that those Group Winners whose group was judged at the beginning of the show have to go back again on the last day to compete for the Best in Show award. Many of the larger show societies provide expenses to cover this eventuality, but in the case of local Open shows this is not to be expected.

A Best in Show is declared at all types of show from Exemption shows upwards, and those who compete are the unbeaten dogs, whether or not they have been in a breed class (for at the smaller shows it is highly likely that they may have been eligible for entry in only an Any Variety class, there being no classes for that specific breed). However, at an Exemption show the Best in Show has to be judged from only the winners of the pedigree classes and the winner is decided before the novelty classes commence.

# Best Puppy awards

At many shows Best Puppy in Breed is also declared. At a small Open show it is likely that there will be only one Puppy class for the breed, but if, for example, the winner of Novice does not exceed twelve months of age and has not been beaten by the Puppy class winner (it need not necessarily have been entered in the Puppy class) then it, too, is eligible to compete for Best Puppy.

At larger shows there may be, for example, Minor Puppy Dog, Puppy Dog, Minor Puppy Bitch and Puppy Bitch classes. In this case all four winners are entitled to compete, as is any puppy unbeaten by another puppy in a higher class, if such exists. If a puppy has won one of the Puppy classes but has been entered and beaten by an adult dog in one of the higher classes, although it relinquishes its right to challenge for Best of Breed or Best of Sex it may still challenge for the Best Puppy award.

# Junior Warrant

The Kennel Club's ruling about Junior Warrants has only recently been changed. Until 1990 a dog had a full twelve months in which to win points which would count towards this award, but now only six months are allowed. The change has been a controversial one, but whatever your viewpoint it is now harder to gain a warrant than it used to be.

To gain a Junior Warrant a dog has to win a total of twenty-five or more points which are allocated on the basis of wins in breed competition at Open and Championship shows. One point is gained for winning a first place at the former and three points for each first gained at the latter, provided that CCs are on offer for the breed. If CCs are not on offer then only one point is gained. Because the points are scored per class, if a dog wins more than one first in the breed at one show he can (if he has a very successful show!) score several points on one day. A first in Junior and, for example, Graduate at a Championship show would amount to six points; at an Open show two first places would give him two points. Formerly a puppy could start collecting points as soon as he went into the show-ring, i.e. from six months onwards, but now the dog has to be twelve months old before he can score such points. What has not changed is that the maximum age for achieving the points is eighteen months. The change that has been made therefore effectively means that a dog has only half the time in which to amass the required number of points, and I know from personal experience that it can be very disappointing to get only twenty-three or twenty-four in the knowledge that there are no shows in the dog's last couple of weeks as a Junior.

The change, though, has met favour with many, especially those involved with the larger breeds where it is not considered in the best interests of the dog to exhibit a youngster other than very occasionally. Indeed, it is a fact that some exhibitors relentlessly dragged their dogs along to each and every possible show from the tender age of six months, purely in the hope of picking up points. Certainly it is true that puppies should not be over-shown for they do get tired with all the travelling and being away from home, which inevitably upsets their routine and eating habits. On the other hand, I feel that young puppies should be taken to some shows so that they learn the ropes and familiarise themselves with the environment of the show-ring and showground, which at first is going to be very strange to them.

Whichever way you look at it, there is, and always has been, a certain element of unfairness in the scoring of points. At some shows and in some breeds there may be very small entries in a class, or even only one entry so that unless the judge chooses to withhold (rare at an Open show) the winner very easily scores one or three points according to the type of show. On the other hand, some breeds have very large entries, especially at Championship shows, and there may be forty or more in a class with still only one winner which gains points towards a Warrant. Geographical location can also make a difference, for more Open show breed classes are available in some areas than in others. To

*Figure 10*

THE KENNEL CLUB

1 CLARGES STREET. LONDON. W1Y 8AB

This is to certify that

LHASA APSO

MODHISH JACK FLASH

has qualified for a

JUNIOR WARRANT

under Kennel Club Rules and Regulations

MISSES J CUNLIFFE & C JOHNSON
LUNDY COTTAGE
PAINSCASTLE
BUILTH WELLS
LD2 3JJ

Registered Owner

Date Issued: 21st. October, 1988.

complicate the system further, whereas a dog used to have a full calendar year in which to earn points, he now has only six months; if those six months fall at the height of the show season there will undoubtedly be more shows available to enter than if the six months span the winter period.

If a dog has been fortunate enough to amass the required number of points, the owner has then to apply to the Kennel Club for the Warrant. This will involve giving an exact listing of all the shows at which the points have been gained, so do be sure to keep a thorough and accurate record for it will be needed. Also don't forget to apply for the Warrant, for if you do not the points your dog has gained will count for nothing in the record books. Junior Warrants which have been claimed and granted are included in a section of the Kennel Club's Stud Book but this does not entitle the dog to a Stud Book Number.

A Junior Warrant is not actually a title, but owners of dogs which have achieved this accolade tend to put the letters JW after the dog's name in advertisements and elsewhere. This cannot, however, be included in show catalogues, so do not mention it when you fill in your entry forms for shows.

## Stud Book entries

To obtain a place in the Kennel Club's Stud Book, and therefore to be allocated a Stud Book Number (SB No.), a dog has to have won a certain placing at a Championship show. Despite the fact that the term 'Stud' is used, bitches may also qualify for entry into the Stud Book in the same manner. The dogs which qualify in this way are, by Kennel Club definition, the following:

- Dogs winning Challenge Certificates or Reserve Challenge Certificates.
- Dogs winning first, second or third prizes in Open or Limit classes where Kennel Club Challenge Certificates are competed for, when such classes are not subject to any limitation as to weight, colour or other description.

There are also other qualifications relating to winners of Field Trials, Working Trials and Obedience competition.

You do not have to write to the Kennel Club for your dog's Stud Book Number when you know that he has qualified for one; it is sent automatically to you by post. Allocation of the Stud Book

THE KENNEL CLUB
1 CLARGES STREET, LONDON, W1Y 8AB

Allocation
of
Stud Book Number

This is to certify that the

LHASA APSO

MODHISH JACK FLASH

has qualified for inclusion in the Kennel Club Stud Book
having been awarded 2nd in Limit Dog at the

MIDLAND LHASA APSO ASSOCIATION

CHAMPIONSHIP SHOW

This dog is now eligible for entry in CRUFTS DOG SHOW
and has been assigned the Stud Book Number

0834BY

J. G. DAVIES
Manager, Awards Dept.

MISSES J CUNLIFFE & C JOHNSON
LUNDY COTTAGE
PAINSCASTLE
BUILTH WELLS
          LD2 3JJ

Date: 23rd. April, 1989.

Registered Owner

An entry to this effect will appear in the Stud Book to be published in June next year.
A Certified List of Awards extracted from the Stud Book for a specific dog is available
by post from the Awards Department or at Crufts Dog Show.

*Figure 11*

Number is sent to you after only the first occasion when your dog qualifies for entry, for thereafter the information has already been recorded and the number allocated does not change. Details of your dog's pedigree, with access to three generations, are also printed in the Stud Book, which is obtainable from the Kennel Club.

# Cruft's qualifiers

Firstly, it must be stressed that qualification to enter Cruft's does not constitute a title of any kind. Also, the Kennel Club does, from time to time, alter the qualifications necessary for entry at their show. This can be done to relieve pressure on an over-crowded venue, as was the case when Puppy and Veteran classes were eliminated, but the new move to the National Exhibition Centre in 1991 means more space, and as a result, the Veteran classes and Special Puppy classes have been reallocated. It is therefore *essential* to check the stipulations for qualification each year, but at its meeting in September 1989 the KC laid down the following qualification for entry at the 1991 show.

For breeds where Challenge Certificates are on offer: Any dog with a Kennel Club Stud Book Number, i.e. that has won a Challenge Certificate, Reserve Challenge Certificate or a First, Second or Third prize in Open and Limit at a Championship Show where Challenge Certificates were on offer for the breed or has qualified for entry in the Stud Book through Field Trials and Working Trials.

Any dog that has won a First, Second or Third prize in Minor Puppy, Puppy, Junior and Post Graduate at a Championship Show where Challenge Certificates were on offer for the breed.

For breeds where Challenge Certificates are not on offer and Any Variety Not Separately Classifed: Any dog that has been declared Best of Sex or Reserve Best of Sex or gained a First, Second or Third prize in Minor Puppy, Puppy, Junior, Post Graduate, Limit and Open (Breed or Variety Classes) at a Championship Show.

Prior to the above regulations being made, second and third prizes in the age classes and in Post Graduate classes did not entitle a dog to enter Cruft's, so you can see that a change of rule on the part of the KC can make a substantial difference to the number of dogs which will, in any one year, be eligible for entry. Qualification for Cruft's is on an annual basis but now that dogs with Stud Book entries are also included, and since they remain in the Stud Book for the rest of their days, they remain permanently eligible for Cruft's – unless, of course, the KC decides to change the qualification for entry yet again!

# Judges

Many people who are newcomers to the world of show dogs and dog shows are somewhat mystified by what, exactly, judges are. Perhaps I can shed a little light on the subject. Basically you will hear of two different types of judge in the UK – 'all-rounders' and 'breed specialists' – and it is generally believed that a breed needs to be judged by a mixture of the two in order to keep a good balance over the years. Any judge should in theory judge to the Kennel Club Breed Standard for any given breed, but very often a breed specialist, being familiar with the finer points of a particular breed, will pay more attention to breed characteristics and breed type, while the all-rounder, understandably often less familiar with breed type, tends to lay greater emphasis on general construction. Showmanship, presentation and handling also often play an especially important part when your dog is being judged by an all-rounder. In having said that I am aware that I have made a very sweeping statement, and naturally one would hope that all judges pay attention to both type and soundness.

Fortunately, there are a number of all-round judges who try to attend specialist breed seminars so that they can become more conversant with the various features of a breed which are considered particular attributes or otherwise by the specialists themselves. However, an all-rounder's time is invariably limited; indeed, some of the country's top all-round judges have an appointment virtually every week and their activities also take them abroad, so it is understandable that they cannot always get to seminars as often as they would like. However, attendance at seminars by all-rounders is always highly appreciated by the specialists involved in running such events.

An all-rounder is someone who judges several different breeds, while a breed specialist, as the term implies, is an expert on her own breed. It is, however, perfectly possible for someone to be considered a breed specialist within their own breed but an all-rounder by exhibitors of other breeds, due to the fact that they judge, as many do, their own breed in addition to others. Some judges like to stand firmly by their own breed and never accept judging appointments for any other, and there are, indeed, people who take pride in the fact that they have been entirely loyal to a breed for fifty years (or more!). Unfortunately, going to the other extreme, there are judges who, over-anxious to further their experience, take on too many breeds too soon. I feel that those judges who wish to judge more than one breed should increase their breeds slowly, thus giving themselves time to study each new breed in depth before tackling it in the ring; in fairness to those who have paid to exhibit under them, this must surely be a necessity.

There are various different categories of judges. The Kennel Club states that each Registered Breed Society must produce a list of judges on an annual basis. The purpose of this list is to indicate to any interested parties which people the Club would support to judge at three different levels, named A, B and C. List A includes the names of all those whom the Club would support to issue Challenge Certificates in the breed and who therefore judge at Championship level and are often referred to as

'Championship show judges'. The breed club need not include the names of all the judges who award CCs in the breed, only those it considers fit to do so. The B list indicates the judges a club would support to judge at Open show level or at a Championship show without CCs on offer for the breed. The C List gives the names of those the Club considers suitable to judge the breed at Limited and Sanction shows. Many clubs have their own additional rules giving specific details about entry on to the list, often stipulating that a person must have judged a certain number of classes or dogs before they can be considered for inclusion. There are cases when, if a club's committee feels that a person is not suitable to be on a list for one reason or another, the name in question is deleted. The Kennel Club recommends that committees prepare their judging lists by secret ballot, but it is up to the individual societies to decide the method by which judges are nominated for the lists. Inclusion on judging lists must not be restricted to members of a society.

You will perhaps appreciate from the above that a judge can be on a club's A list for one breed and on a different club's B or C list for another. It is also perfectly possible for a person to be on the A list with one breed club and the B list, or even not on any list at all, with another club within the same breed. Some breeds try to keep a degree of uniformity by forming a breed council. This means that either all or the majority of clubs for that particular breed get together for various purposes, one of which is to compile a joint list of judges. Some breed societies and breed councils also make it a rule that judges included on the lists must have passed a certain examination set by them. It has to be said that in a few breeds the stipulations made prior to inclusion are almost unbelievably stiff, stating how many years and how many classes (sometimes even a hundred or more) a person must have judged after passing the exam, and how many dogs they have bred or owned which are entered in the Kennel Club Stud Book. A further stipulation sometimes made is that the judge applying for inclusion must have judged at least two breed club shows, and the appointment is offered as a result of a ballot by club members. So, as you can see, for some breeds at least, inclusion on a judging list is no mean feat.

The purpose of breed clubs' and breed councils' judging lists is that they can be sent to Championship show societies and to Secretaries of other shows upon request. This then helps these societies to select judges who are felt to be competent to judge at the level indicated, and this in turn should mean that those societies which invite judges from clubs and council lists get good support from exhibitors, therefore resulting in good entries at their shows.

Although there are no guidelines set down indicating how new judges should begin, most start as breed specialists, perhaps judging their own breed at Limited and Open show level before, if they wish and are invited to do so, spreading their wings to cover other breeds as well. Some may have the opportunity to judge a Match or an Exemption show at the beginning of their judging career and this can give them experience in a cross-section of breeds without the strain of a formal show at which exhibitors have paid a fair sum for the benefit of their opinion. New judges must, however, realise that even at Match and Exemption show level people are spending their valuable time and so it is important that no judge accepts any appointment too lightly.

Breed specialists judging at Championship level will already have judged the breed for a good many years before they are able to award Challenge Certificates, for in order to do so they have to be approved by the Kennel Club. Prior to making a decision the Kennel Club contacts the breed clubs or breed councils for their opinions and considers these in conjunction with the following factors:

- Length and depth of judging experience. In general the Kennel Club will expect an overall judging experience of five years before the date of the proposed appointment.
- The Open shows judged.
- Whether the proposed judge has already judged a breed club Limited or Open show for the breed concerned.
- The dogs bred and/or owned by the proposed judge.
- The proposed judge's overall judging experience.
- All other circumstances which the Kennel Club's Judges Sub-Committee may consider appropriate.

Thus you will see that all Championship show judges who award Challenge Certificates have to have undergone a long and stringent apprenticeship.

An all-rounder sometimes does not have quite such a long background in judging a particular breed before awarding CCs for the first time, but offset against that is the fact that she has substantial experience in judging one or more other breeds at Championship level.

As mentioned earlier, some judges will have passed judging examinations for the breeds they judge, these having been organised by the various breed clubs. However, in many cases judges are invited to officiate even though they have not taken such an exam and, indeed, in some breeds no such examinations exist. Judging examinations are a relatively new innovation in the UK's canine world and certainly the training of judges and prospective judges is an aspect of the dog scene which the Kennel Club encourages. The various examinations take many different forms, some being purely practical while others involve a written examination too. In many cases the examinees are obliged to attend certain seminars before they may apply to take the exam. Some judges also hold the Canine Studies Institute's Judging Diploma which is awarded following successful completion of a course designed, in particular, to help all-rounders, although it is also undoubtedly of benefit to breed specialists. The CSI Diploma course takes several months to complete and covers, in substantial depth, all aspects of judging, also involving attendance at a number of seminars which are spread over the period of study.

Always bear in mind that the judge standing in the centre of the ring has almost invariably at some time or other also been an exhibitor, so he knows exactly what it feels like to be in your position. Many judges, especially the breed specialists, continue to exhibit throughout their judging careers, and often someone who judges only one breed carries out, on average, just one appointment each year, or even less at Championship level because the Kennel Club and show societies stipulate that there must be a given period between appointments. As a result it is quite possible that the person who judges you at a show one week will be standing next to you in the ring with his dog the next. If it should happen that your neighbour in the ring is the person who is due to judge your dog the following week, remember that it is not considered good form to advise the person concerned that you have entered your dog under her, and it is certainly not done to point out your dog's good points, while to draw attention to his bad ones would be plain foolish. Such things do happen, but most judges worth their salt simply ignore any comments made and judge as they see fit on the day.

# Group judges at Championship shows

The minimum standard generally required by the Kennel Club is that a Group judge must already award Challenge Certificates in at least three different breeds within the group. For a Working Group judge the minimum number of breeds is four. The prospective judge should have an overall judging experience of no less than seven years and all-round judging experience at Open show level is also to be taken into account, as is experience in other groups.

# Best in Show judges at Championship level

The Kennel Club tells us that generally speaking the requirements for a Best in Show judge are that he or she has a sound general knowledge of dogs and a real competence as a judge. A Best in Show judge should be qualified to judge at least one Group as well as to award Challenge Certificates to some breeds in other groups. All-round judging experience at Open shows is also taken into account.

The Kennel Club stresses that, notwithstanding the above stipulations, the approval of persons to judge at Championship shows is the sole prerogative of the Kennel Club's General Committee.

# Scope of judges

In the case of Championship shows it is again the Kennel Club which stipulates how many dogs a judge can handle in one day. The KC recognises that overloading a judge can lead to serious problems at Championship show level and in consequence it does not allow one judge to officiate for more than three breeds on one day, except in very exceptional circumstances. In fairness both to the judge and to the exhibitors, the Committee will reallocate a breed to another judge if, when entries close, the following numbers are exceeded:

| | |
|---|---|
| One breed: | Up to 250 dogs |
| Two breeds: | Up to 200 dogs |
| Three breeds: | Up to 175 dogs |

# Contact with judges

It has already been mentioned that it is not accepted as good form to comment to a forthcoming judge that you have entered your dog under her and that she is sure to like particularly his good shoulder placement, excellent front, or whatever. In addition to this, a judge can be put in an awkward position by a novice exhibitor who asks them to go over their dog to assess his merits and perhaps his faults at a time when they are not judging. This is all well and good most of the time, but don't be offended if a judge says that she would prefer not to do so. This may be because they will be judging in the relatively near future and therefore would prefer to reserve judgement on your dog in case you enter under them. After all, if the person concerned pulls your dog to pieces you will probably choose not to enter under her, whereas if she says that she especially likes your dog she may wonder if you feel she is saying that in order to gain your entry at the next show. If a judge does go over your dog in an 'unofficial' capacity and makes favourable comments, there is naturally a reasonable chance that she will like your dog if ever she does judge it. But even though she may like your dog, whether or not he gains an award will depend upon the way he performs and looks on the day and, very importantly, the strength of the competition in his class.

When exhibiting your dog the motto is not to enter into conversation with the judge unless the judge instigates the discussion. While the judge is going over your dog she will wish to concentrate on the job in hand, not discuss the intricacies of the weather. And certainly don't point out your dog's assets to the judge; worse still, never point out his bad points. You don't have to apologise for a dog's bad mouth or crooked front; the judge will weigh those points against his better ones, and if you are very lucky she may not think they are quite as bad as you do, so don't bring her attention to them. Believe me, I've seen this happen far more frequently than you might imagine – you would be surprised what some exhibitors say to judges!

When judging is completed many novice exhibitors have an urge to go up to the judge to ask what she thought of their dog. In actual fact, the judge has expressed what she thought of the dog by the placing she awarded to it in the class. Just bear in mind that judges often have to work to a fairly tight schedule, especially if they are all-rounders, so if you really feel you must ask a question it will undoubtedly be appreciated if you keep it short. Gone are the days when judges went round the benches after judging to discuss various points with the exhibitors, and many lament the passing of those times. Do not expect a judge to remember exactly what she liked or disliked about your dog for she will have gone over up to 250 dogs on the day and cannot possibly be expected to remember everything about every one of them.

Many breed specialists are only too willing to help novice exhibitors when time permits, so you would probably be much better advised to approach them after the event, on another occasion, giving them the opportunity to see your dog again and asking if they would be kind enough to make constructive comments to help you learn more about your dog. Above all, do *not* follow the judge into the loo during the lunch break so that you can pester with questions while in the queue or at the wash-hand basin – I've had it happen to me on more than one occasion, and frankly it is simply not appreciated!

# 7

# Learning more about dogs

If you are going to get the best out of your dog when showing him, you need to know what the judges are looking for and so you must learn as much as you possibly can about the breed. After all, one day you may want to take a dog of your own breeding into the show-ring and you will want to have picked up as much information as possible about the breed so that you know what you are aiming for in your breeding programme. Apart from the fact that your knowledge will enable you to show your dog to the best advantage and will undoubtedly help you if you ever become a breeder, having a thorough knowledge and understanding of the breed will make your show days much more pleasurable for you will appreciate the breed with which you have decided to become involved.

You probably got into conversation with some of the major breeders when you were looking for your puppy, and if you have been lucky you will have bought from someone who not only shows the breed herself but also takes an interest in the dogs she sells to other exhibitors. If so, you will at least have a contact at shows and someone to turn to if you need advice. Do, however, keep your horizons wide and get into conversation with as many exhibitors as you can, for you will find that virtually everyone has a slightly differing opinion – indeed, dog showing would be a very boring pastime if everyone thought that the same dog was the best.

The sad fact is that many people spend many years 'in dogs' without actually learning very much about them. Please don't become one of them or you will miss out on a great deal of the pleasure which can be derived from the canine world. Many people declare that one either has or has not got a good eye for a dog. To a certain extent this is true, but however good or bad your natural eye you can learn to develop it, although you must go about this the right way.

As you converse with fellow exhibitors you will be suprised at how much constructive information you acquire. Do not, however, take everything that is said as 'gospel', but learn to listen patiently to what is being said and then make your own assessment of whether or not you agree. You will almost undoubtedly find that your own opinions will change as you learn more and gain more experience of seeing the breed around you. Beware of the know-it-alls. Nobody knows everything, even if they have been successfully involved in a breed for many years, and those who really understand their breed will, I feel sure, admit to that. People to beware of especially are those who have had a breed for a couple of years, had a few minor wins, probably at local show level, and who then try to take you under their wing, often appearing like old hands to you, the newcomer. This seems to give them a bit of an ego trip and they frequently go overboard in imparting their advice, which is not always as sound as it might be. I say again that eventually it is for you to make up your own mind about the breed, and if you keep your eyes and ears carefully open you will soon know whose advice to seek and whose opinions you can respect.

If you are especially lucky some people may let you go over their dogs when explaining a point and this will give you an opportunity to learn more from 'hands-on' experience, an excellent way to learn. Do, however, be cautious about any comments you make and if faults are kindly pointed out to you by the owner of the dog in question, don't pass on these comments to others; that would simply not be playing the game.

## From the ring-side

There is a lot you can do yourself at a show without being a bother to other people who, you must always remember, have their own dogs to groom and exhibit and so may not have very much time to spare with you. Take a seat by the ring-side (it's always a good idea to take along a picnic chair for seats can be few and far between) and watch carefully every exhibit in turn. If you have chosen your place with care you will have managed to find a spot where you can select a particular aspect to study on the day. In the smaller breeds a seat near the judging table will probably give you a good view of the dog's finer points as the judge goes over it. Alternatively, you can position yourself so that you are in line with the dog as he moves for the judge, which will help you to learn to assess what is correct and what incorrect as far as movement in your particular breed is concerned.

Carefully watch the exhibitors, too, so that you can pick up tips from those who show their dogs well. See how the experienced ones deal with problems such as strong wind, over-crowding and pot-holes in the grass. You may have noticed a dog which is, for example, a little longer in loin than is ideal; note how the experienced handler stands him at a very slight angle to the judge so that his length is not accentuated. Watch how, when asked to move round the ring together at the beginning of a class, the better handlers make one hundred per cent certain that their dogs are not being crowded and are moving at their very best pace just as they come into the judge's line of view. Learn, too, from the exhibitors who don't handle so well. If you see something that is not helping a dog, make a mental note that you will endeavour not to make that mistake yourself. Look at colour co-ordination. If there are dogs of a similar colour to your own, against which colour clothes do they seem to show up best? The variety of things you can learn from your ring-side vantage point is endless.

# Movement

Earlier we mentioned that to make the best of your dog you should move him at the pace which is correct for him. Let us now look at movement in a little more depth, for by understanding the various faults in movement you should be able to practise with your dog so that you are minimising the faults which can be seen by the judge. Naturally, if your dog has a construction fault which affects his movement you will never be able to make the fault go away. You may, however, be able to avoid getting your dog into situations where it shows up more strongly.

Another factor which must be taken into consideration is that, of course, the various breeds of dog are constructed differently, and movement which is correct for one breed might be totally incorrect for another. To cite two extreme examples, let us look at the sections of the Breed Standards which concern movement for the Bulldog and for the Saluki.

*Learn to move your dog at the pace which is best for him*

*Bulldog* Gait/Movement peculiarly heavy and constrained, appearing to walk with short, quick steps on tips of toes, hind feet not lifted high, appearing to skim ground, running with one or other shoulder rather advanced.

Such movement would cause a Saluki owner to have a fit, but it is perfectly correct for the Bulldog due to the way in which the breed is constructed. Have a look at the Breed Standard for the Bulldog and you will find that it differs greatly in all respects from that of the Saluki. Take, for example, the fact that the fore legs are to be set wide apart and that they are to 'present rather a bowed outline', not that the bones themselves are to be other than straight, but you can see immediately that the construction contrasts strongly with the Saluki whose chest is to be 'deep and moderately narrow' and whose fore legs are to be 'straight and long from elbow to wrist'. Then compare the following description with that which you have just read above.

*Saluki* Gait/Movement light, lifting, effortless, showing both reach and drive, body lifting off ground with long flat strides, not flinging itself forward. No hackney action or plodding.

*This Saluki has won Best of Breed and is now in competition in the Hound group. Clearly the handler knows how to present her to perfection*

I did say that the two examples are extreme, but I hope that they suffice to give you some indication of how movement can, and must, differ from breed to breed. You will therefore appreciate that it would be impossible to go into movement for each specific breed in a book of this nature (just as it is simply not possible to describe grooming techniques for all breeds), but you should find that, with practice, you can study your own breed and determine which dogs are moving well and which are moving incorrectly. You will also notice that certain faults are exaggerated or minimised according to the speed at which the dog is taken.

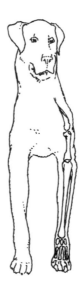

*Figure 12    In repose the pad is in a direct line below the centre of the shoulder blade.*

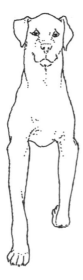

*Figure 13    When the dog is moving slowly the legs are still in an almost vertical line.*

Firstly, it is important to know that the faster a dog moves, the more he is inclined to single track. This means that as speed increases the pads converge towards a central line, as you will be able to see in the diagram. This is perfectly correct, for it is a natural movement. If you have the opportunity to do so, watch your dog's tracks as he moves faster and faster through snow and you will see how the prints made by his pads grow closer together. However, some breeds, especially rather broad, short-legged ones, are not capable of single tracking to the same degree as the longer-legged dogs, but the legs will nevertheless incline to a certain extent.

*Figure 14 At the trot there is still a straight line from shoulder to pad but the line is now inclining inwards.*

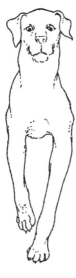

*Figure 15 When moving at speed, although the legs are still in a straight line, they incline inwards still further but do not touch as each foot is flexed in turn.*

*What to look for when a dog is moving toward you*

As a dog moves toward you you will, in several cases, see movement as similar to that described above as is possible within the confines of the dog's breed. However, you will also notice many faults.

Perhaps one of the most common faults is TOEING IN, also known as WEAVING, PLAITING or KNITTING AND PURLING. In such movement the front feet cross over as they move toward you in a criss-cross pattern. Such movement is often coupled with a dog being out at elbow. See Figures 16 and 17.

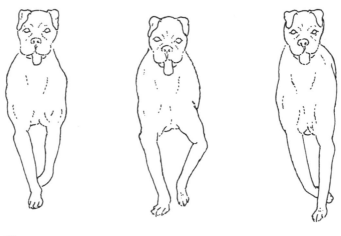

*Figure 16*

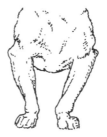

*Figure 17*

Being out at elbow can also cause a dog to PADDLE which is an energy wasting movement in which the pasterns and feet make a circular movement, flicking outwards at the end of each step. See Figure 18.

*Figure 18*

Another problem which can be seen easily is when a dog moves WIDE IN FRONT, often caused by an incorrect ribcage and as can be seen in Figure 19.

*Figure 19*

## *As the dog moves in profile*

As each exhibit moves across the top of the ring in profile you will notice some which OVER REACH, usually caused because the hind angulation is too great for the angulation of the forequarters, which, in turn, means that the dog is not well balanced. This can be seen in Figure 20.

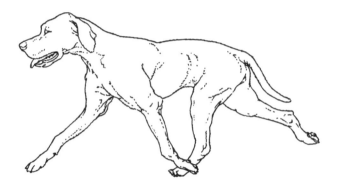

*Figure 20*

*Figure 21*

Figure 21 shows a HACKNEY ACTION which may be correct in a breed such as the Miniature Pinscher but in most breeds it is a fault. The term is taken from the hackney horse and is characterised by an exaggerated lift of the feet, especially in the forequarters but also in the hindquarters to a lesser degree.

*Figure 22*

Another movement which is considered a fault in the show ring is PACING. If you have one of the short backed breeds you may find that your dog has a tendency to pace, as shown in Figure 22. This means that he moves both his right legs and then both his left ones in order to avoid leg interference due, usually, to a 'square' structural shape. This brings with it a tendency to roll from side to side as the weight is shifted from one side to the other. Practice will help you to avoid your dog pacing when in the show ring.

## Moving away

One of the major faults you will observe as a dog moves away from you is MOVING CLOSE BEHIND as showwn in Figure 23 *(left)* and in which the back legs (especially from the hock joint downwards) are too close together, sometimes even causing them to brush against one another. Another fault frequently to be seen is COW HOCKS in which the hocks incline inwards and in which case the hocks themselves tend to brush together as the dog

*Figure 23*

*Figure 24*

*Figure 25*

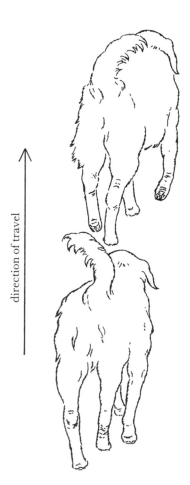

direction of travel

moves. This form of gait severely restricts freedom of movement and can be seen in Figure 23 *(right)*.

A dog which moves WIDE BEHIND can also be called 'bandy' or 'bow hocked' and an example of this can be seen in Figure 24.

CRABBING is another incorrect gait which can be observed from all angles but initially you will perhaps observe it most easily when viewed from behind. Caused most often by a dog having greater angulation in the rear than in the forequarters the hind legs move forward to one side, rather than in a direct line, to avoid the back legs interfering with the front ones as he moves. The expression is taken from the movement of a sea crab and in the dog it is an awkward and inefficient gait shown in Figure 25. This, especially, is one of the faults in movement which can be exaggerated, or even caused, by poor handling. If your dog does have a tendency to crab it is a habit which can take a long time to break. To stop this habit choose a very quiet road and practise walking him along the very edge of the pavement so that he is encouraged to move in a straight line with all four feet, otherwise he will simply end up with his hind feet in the gutter. This usually works and the training can be continued in the ring (at an indoor show at least) by moving him along the very edge of the mat, which he will most probably associate with the curb on which he has been practising. The sooner you start to remedy this fault the easier it will be.

## How the lead can hinder and help

Many exhibitors tend to 'string up' their dogs but this is not always to good effect and can be positively detrimental. Many of the older generation of judges positively abhor dogs being shown on a tight lead and, once an exhibitor has moved her dog once in this way, the judge will clearly instruct the exhibitor to 'move him again, on a loose lead please'.

Basically, if the lead is strung too tightly the dog's front movement will be restricted, there are cases where the feet hardly seem to touch the ground and it can certainly tend to make the dog cross in front more than he might otherwise do. This is shown in Figure 26. If the dog pulls away from you whilst on the move, again, causing a tight lead, this again will accentuate a tendency to cross (Figure 27) and can also cause him to crab. Whichever way you choose to hold your dog's lead, and this will vary according to the breed to a certain extent as will the pace at which

Figure 26

Figure 27

you take him, both you and the dog need to be moving in exactly the same direction.

If your dog constantly moves too close to you, this can most probably be remedied by allowing him a little more lead and, on the contrary, if you wish him to move closer in you will find that, with a flick of the wrist, you can wind the lead round your fingers just a few inches more and this will make all the difference without having to alter the stride. Bear in mind always that a dog will respond much more readily to a short, sharp jerk on the lead rather than a steady pull, which will probably make matters worse rather than better.

## Learning from other breeds

I am not here suggesting that you watch only your own breed at shows, for there is a lot to be learned from other breeds, too. My advice is that you should watch your own breed as much as possible but in those few spare moments after judging is complete, or during the lunch break, take yourself off to watch one of the other breeds for in this way you will not allow yourself to become blinkered, with eyes only for those of your own kind.

It is surprising how you will be able to pick out from the ringside the experienced handlers who are really making the most of their dogs. A good handler can get the best out of virtually any dog of any breed, although I think all experienced exhibitors recognise that some dogs are more difficult to handle than others. You will soon get to know some of the 'famous names' in dogs and, if you can find the opportunity to do so, watch them handle different breeds; you will see that they adapt their handling style to suit not only the breed but also the dog in question (although the latter may not always be so easily observed).

If you are at a Championship show, towards the end of the day try to find half an hour to watch the Group judging. This will be announced over the tannoy system and it should be easy to find the ring because it is generally the one with the most activity surrounding it at that time of day. Here you will see all the handlers with dogs that have been declared Best of Breed, so the chances are that most of these people are experienced exhibitors who are able to show their dogs to best advantage. Of course, there can be occasions when novice exhibitors' dogs are declared Best of Breed, but even in such cases there is every chance that they are handling their dogs well on the day so you can learn from them too – unless, of course, it is you who is the lucky novice exhibitor who finds herself in the 'big ring'. Believe me, it does happen!

While watching this bevy of clever handlers, look out also for the few dogs which are put off by the 'big ring' situation and see how their handlers come to terms with the problems encountered so that they make the best of the situation. The chances are that all the dogs you see before you in the Group behaved well in their breed judging, otherwise it is unlikely that they would have been declared Best of Breed. However, especially at indoor shows where there are strong lights and often an unfamiliar floor surface, dogs can behave quite differently in the Group, which is terribly disappointing for the owners. It may be that, due partly to the surroundings which have somewhat overawed them, they decide to take an instant dislike to the judge, backing off on the floor or table as she is examining them. Watch how the handlers try to calm the dogs and give them confidence; watch, too, how they do not allow themselves to be rushed. Take careful note in all respects and you will find that something which you have observed will sooner or later be of assistance to you with your own exhibit.

## Study critiques

The majority of judges write a critique after a show and these are reported in the dog press, often a few weeks after the event. You will find an index of show critiques in the paper, but having located the show in question, don't despair if the breed you are particularly looking for doesn't appear immediately, for you will find that some breeds appear one week, some the next, depending largely upon when the judge wrote her report. Of course, if you have won you will want to look at the judge's comments about your own dog, but don't confine your interest in critiques to only those shows at which you have won. Read all the reports and see if any of the comments made about the various dogs tie in with your own opinions from the ring-side.

If you look carefully at show reports you will be surprised at how different critiques written about the same dogs vary. If you know what you are looking for in the reports, this will often give you a clue as to which are the better judges. Of course, no one can judge a breed completely from the ring-side but you can, for example, see that a short-coated dog which is meant to have a straight front has a bowed one. If a judge says that that same dog has 'good shoulders and front' or 'soundly constructed forehand', you know that either the dog has magically improved or the judge did not notice his obvious fault.

The terminology given in Chapter 10 will help you to understand critiques a little more easily. You must also bear in mind when reading them that many judges do not like to write too critically about a dog in a report which is for all to read. You are probably wondering why a judge should even need to consider writing critically about a dog which she has placed first or second. The reason is that in many cases, especially in classes with small entries, a judge does not really find a dog which she feels is of high quality yet the dog may not be so poor that the placing should be withheld. Alternatively, it is possible that the judge does not agree with withholding prize cards, in which case when writing a report she will often try to find the attributes rather than the negative points to describe in the critique. A report which mentions that a dog has an abundance of coat and is well handled but gives no praise of any structural point probably implies that all is not what it might be under the coat. 'Preferred size of one above' most probably indicates that the second-place winner was either too large or too small, though the judge has written the critique rather more tactfully.

If you can find the time and if you have the patience it is a good idea to cut out and paste into a scrapbook all the Championship show reports you find about your own breed. This is especially interesting to keep and look back on from time to time, especially when you are perhaps thinking of selecting a stud dog for your bitch. If you have admired a potential stud dog from the ring-side but find that eight out of ten judges have indicated that he has an incorrect bite, for example, you may decide to cross him off your list, especially if something you wish to improve upon in the next generation is the bite.

You will most probably want to keep a copy of all your own dog's show reports but if, as I suggest, you keep *all* the reports you can highlight those about your own dog so that you can see the comments made in perspective. This will, I assure you, teach you much more in the long run.

# Seminars

By now you should have become a member of one or more breed clubs and there is a good chance that they will run occasional seminars. These are often called 'teach-ins' and can sometimes be described as 'judging seminars'. Don't be put off by the latter description for in many cases even those who are new to the breed are welcome to attend the seminar to learn more. Just give a courtesy call to the organiser so that you are sure you will be welcome and will not feel out of place. Some clubs have one or more seminars each year which are open to everyone, often including non-members, and then one or more smaller sessions which are open only to candidates for the breed's judging exams –something with which you need not concern yourself at this early stage. I cannot stress strongly enough that at the outset of your involvement in dog showing you should concentrate on learning to show your dog well and absorbing as much information as you can about the breed. Judging is something which will take its natural course, all in good time. If you are learning as much as you can about the breed now, that will stand you in good stead later on if judging invitations are extended to you. If you have shown interest and enthusiasm in the breed, especially by attending seminars, this will undoubtedly be noticed by those who are responsible for suggesting new people as prospective judges. Certainly don't try to push yourself into that side of the dog world at this early stage for you will be doing neither the breed nor yourself any favours. The newer exhibitors who are most highly thought of by the people who matter are those who take the breed seriously, exhibit regularly, are considerate to their dogs and don't rush too quickly into breeding or judging. Those who take on judging appointments too soon will probably make some fundamental blunders which will be noticed by other, more experienced judges, the result being that their reputations as judges will be hindered rather than helped and subsequent appointments will not be as readily forthcoming as the first.

Besides seminars run by your own breed society, watch out in the canine press for those run by other clubs. Often a club which covers an entire group has seminars covering different breeds each year and on such occasions specialist speakers are usually invited. Often you do not have to be a member of the club to attend such lectures and the fee charged is rarely more than

*Seminars can be informative and pleasurable too. Often the organising club's committee arranges a super lunch which helps to make the event a real social occasion*

sufficient to cover the cost of hiring the venue, with perhaps a buffet lunch. When attending such seminars you will find it useful to take along appropriate copies of the Kennel Club's Breed Standards for they are not always handed out at the seminar. It is also a good idea to make notes on the Standard as the speaker makes reference to certain points, and never feel shy about getting out your Standard or making notes. All of us need to check things from time to time, even concerning the breeds with which we are supposedly thoroughly familiar. I recently attended a seminar where both the speaker and some well-established exhibitors in a certain breed insisted that there was no Temperament clause in their Standard; had I not had my Breed Standard with me I might have been unwittingly misled for there was, in fact, such a clause. You will not, of course, want to carry a heavy book around with you, so send off to the Kennel Club for the current Breed Standard leaflet, at least for your own Group; it will cost you a very small sum and you can be sure that it will be up to date (Breed Standards do change from time to time). The Kennel Club occasionally has a stand at major shows and certainly at Cruft's, where these and other useful leaflets can be purchased.

Seminars, sometimes of a longer nature, are arranged also by professional organisations and some of these may include specific lectures about or relating to your own breed. The cost of these is generally somewhat higher than those run by canine societies, partly because they also include overnight accommodation, but they can be most informative and are an excellent way of meeting other people who are as interested in the canine species as you are. Don't worry if you have no one to go along with you to such seminars; you are unlikely to feel out of place on your own as you can almost guarantee that there will be others who are lacking a companion with such a deep interest in learning.

# Stewarding

Not during your very early days as an exhibitor but when you are fully conversant with ring procedure, you may wish to consider offering your services as a steward, perhaps at one of the small local shows. Naturally you must have watched good stewards working in the ring for a long while before you make such an offer, but stewarding can provide the opportunity to acquire a good deal of knowledge at grass-roots level. A disadvantage, of course, is that you cannot realistically show your own breed and steward under the same judge, but you may, for example, have been lucky enough to have been awarded a Best of Breed by a certain judge and thus you would not, if you follow the usually accepted exhibiting ethics, take that same dog under the same judge again, which leaves you free to offer to steward.

If you really feel that you are sufficiently conversant with procedure, you should contact the show organisers and offer to help out as an assistant steward; this will mean that you will be in the ring with someone more experienced than you. While stewarding for a judge some discussion with her will inevitably be necessary, but I would urge you not to enter into deep convers-ation nor to pester with questions. This does not look good to the ring-siders and can be most off-putting for the judge whose prime purpose is to appraise the dogs placed under her; your job as steward is to assist the judge in the course of her duties. I once recall judging when a steward insisted on asking why I had placed the dogs in my chosen order at the end of every class. It was clear that she was simply trying to learn more about a breed which was new to her, but I have to admit that it took a great deal of effort on my part to keep my patience. Please don't be one of those infuriating stewards who distract the judge rather than assist her.

The Kennel Club rules state clearly that stewards should always remember that the judge is in overall control of the ring and that they should follow the judge's directives. It is, however, the steward's responsibility to ensure the smooth and efficient running of the ring. Basically, if you do act as a steward it will be your job to ensure that all material is provided in the ring for posting of awards and that all prize cards for each class are readily available. You will also be responsible for taking 'reasonable steps' to see that exhibitors are aware when judging is due to commence and to make sure not only that every exhibitor in each class is wearing a ring number but that it is the correct one. It is surprising how many times one marks down the awards at the end of a class only to find that such and such a number wasn't even entered in that class. This is usually a simple slip on the part of the exhibitor who is showing more than one dog on the day, but in actual fact the steward should have checked all ring numbers thoroughly before commencement of judging for that class. Sometimes the exhibitors will have collected their ring numbers from their benches or from the Secretary's table, but on other occasions, especially at smaller shows, the steward hands out the appropriate numbers as the exhibitors enter the ring, checking them off against the numbers in the catalogue as he does so.

The steward also has to see to it that the only dogs present in the ring are those which are being judged, and, if the judge requests him to do so, to place those dogs which have been seen in previous classes in the order of their awards. Once this has been done the steward should advise the judge that all dogs are present, having marked off the absentees, for at the end of the show the Kennel Club will wish to be advised by the show society not only which dogs have been placed but also which were absent on the day. At this point Kennel Club instructions state that the steward should 'retire to a corner of the Ring and subsequently only converse with the Judge if requested to perform a specific duty'. I think that statement speaks for itself.

While judging is in progress the steward should ensure that

dogs near the ring or around the ring-side do not interfere with the exhibits which are being judged, and he should also ensure that photographers are not in the ring while judging is in progress. In addition, he is to see to it that 'double handling' does not occur. This means that no one outside the ring should be trying to attract the attention of the dog inside it, a habit which has become prevalent in some breeds but which is strictly prohibited. If, as a steward, you are unlucky enough to see this happening, it will be your duty to report it to the judge and it will be for her to take appropriate action.

Upon completion of judging in each class the steward should, technically, remind the judge to place the dogs in descending order from left to right, although it is a poor judge indeed who needs to be reminded of this. Prize cards and any other prizes should be given out by the steward and awards should be clearly marked or posted on the award board, which is usually situated in a corner of the ring. Correctly marked slips should be signed by the judge and sent to the Show Secretary's or Show Manager's Office, and in the case of Championship shows it is for the steward to see to it that the Challenge and Reserve Challenge Certificates are signed by the judge and the correct numbers of the winners entered in the judging book.

So, as you can see, as a steward you will be busy for quite a large proportion of the time that you are in the ring, but none the less, if you are stewarding for a competent judge at a well-run show with not too many problems caused by exhibitors with incorrect entries and suchlike, you should have a good while during each class to watch the dogs in the ring. This you will be able to do from close quarters without the distraction of conversing with fellow exhibitors, and if you watch carefully you will probably learn a lot. Be careful, however, not to neglect your work as a steward because you are so involved with watching the breed. You are there as a steward to 'assist the judge' and not for your own benefit, so make sure that your first priority is your duty as a steward; any experience you gain as a result should be a bonus.

## Newsletters and magazines

You will hear it said by many that practical experience is much more valuable than learning from books, but my opinion is that the two should go hand in hand. Many of the older breeders had a great deal of sound advice to offer, but these days many are sadly no longer with us to impart their knowledge. Seek out whatever old breed club newsletters you can lay your hands on – you may find back issues for sale at club shows or on breed club stands at Cruft's, or you can approach club Secretaries to ask if they can send you back numbers for a small fee; most will be pleased to help if spares are available. You will often find that some of the old-timers in your breed have written articles in these newsletters, or they may perhaps have been interviewed by the editor and their comments have thus made their way on to the printed page. Sometimes at breed club shows there is a bring-and-buy stall to raise money for club funds, and it is surprising what interesting information some people throw out to make a bit more shelf space. But be sure to take a look at the stand early in the day, preferably before judging starts, otherwise you will find that if there was anything of interest it will already have been snapped up.

Other places where you may be able to seek out old material are the rescue stands at shows, and not necessarily the rescue stand for your own breed, for all sorts of magazines, including back issues of the very informative *Kennel Gazette*, are donated to such a worthy cause and in these old magazines you may just find a valuable article about your very own breed, a treasure to be sure.

# Books

In addition, of course, there are books. They come in all shapes and sizes and the talents and knowledge of the various writers differ greatly, so do select with care. At the major Championship shows you will always find a couple of stalls which specialise in modern canine publications and you will perhaps be surprised to see just how many dog books there are on the shelves. You will probably find that you would like to buy at least a dozen or so books, but finances may be limited and in any case you need to find the time to read them. Select, therefore, with care, choosing a book which deals either only with your breed or with a small handful of breeds, rather than one which covers perhaps a hundred plus. In the latter case you will undoubtedly find very little information about your own specific breed. If you don't get to many major shows to look at the books on display, you will frequently find lists of specialist books for sale in the canine press and many of these can be obtained by mail order. If you live in one of the large cities you may also find a fair selection of breed books at the major book stores, but don't be tempted to buy one of the cheap issues which has been produced for a mass market for it will probably not give you very much information about your own breed and that which it does give may not be as accurate as you would hope.

It is always worth looking at the second-hand and antiquarian canine booksellers, too. You will usually find one or more such stands at the major Championship shows and prices often are not as high as you might imagine; certainly a well-bound first edition can cost well into three figures but if you are content to make do with a less pristine copy or, perhaps, a fifth edition of a not so rare book, you should get away with spending very much less. At dog shows the specialist booksellers are always ready to help you find the book of your choice, and the real enthusiasts can tell you exactly what information is contained in any specific book. Do, though, treat all books on the shelves with the very greatest care; some of them have been around for very many years and are not simply stock items which can be replaced if damaged. You will always find the cost of old books marked in pencil on the first or second page, so if, as you open the book, you notice that it is one of the very valuable ones, please handle it with the care it deserves.

You will be lucky if your small local library has in stock a wealth of material concerning your own chosen breed, but a visit to one of the major branches may produce a better selection. You can, of course, also order a book through your library upon payment of a small fee. You may not be able to get hold of some of the privately printed books in this manner but those published by major companies can usually be obtained, even though you may have to wait a few weeks. If you love books as much as I do you will never be happy until the book of your choice is sitting comfortably and permanently on your bookshelf, in which case you will find that you build up a worthwhile collection as the years progress.

## Look to the future

Those of you who have taken a special interest in this chapter are probably the ones who are, by now, very aware that you still have a great deal to learn and that your first show dog is not a perfect specimen. Take consolation in the fact that the perfect dog has not yet been bred, and as you go on learning you will come to know what you are aiming for in the future. After all, sooner or later you may decide to have a second show dog, and with the knowledge you have gained thus far you will be in a much better position not only to select but also to train your next dog correctly from the outset.

# 8

# After your dog has
# been judged

You have trained your show dog, prepared it for exhibition, taken it to a show, and judging of your breed or the classes you have entered is now complete. The day, for you, has already reached its climax in terms of exhibiting your dog. You may have won or you may have lost, but at the end of the day you still have what, in your own estimation, is the best dog there, the one which lives as your companion and shares your hearth. Whatever the judge thought of him on the day should not alter your opinion of your dog, for you are still taking home the same much-loved animal with which you went to the show that morning. You may, as your days as an exhibitor have progressed, have come to be aware of many of his faults and, indeed, many of his virtues, too, but whichever outweighs the other you should think none the less highly of him as a companion.

Whether or not he has been placed, when his class is complete you should always give him plenty of praise for he will be well aware of your feelings and if he has not been placed you do not want your disappointment at losing to travel down the lead to him. It is surprising how much of your own pent-up emotion can make itself felt through that lead, so try not to let him feel too much. After all, he probably doesn't mind in the least whether or not he got pulled out into the middle of the ring at the end of his class! Showing must always be made a pleasure for your dog. A dog which is never given encouragement is hardly likely to enjoy his outing and this will show in his ring presence, so lack of praise will not only make for an unhappy dog but will also spoil your chances of winning with him. A judge can usually spot an unhappy exhibit a mile off, so always try your utmost to keep him happy and alert throughout the day.

Don't forget that your dog still needs and deserves attention after he has been put through his paces in the ring; don't be one of those exhibitors who put their dog back on his bench or in his crate and then leave him there for hours without so much as a second look. Your dog should always be offered a drink when he comes out of the ring, especially so on a hot summer's day. Always be sure that your water container is handy so that you can offer refreshment as often as necessary. Many dogs seem not to want to accept a drink at shows, but they must always be given the opportunity to drink if they wish and if you do have one of the reluctant ones it is always a good idea at least to moisten his lips. If you have one of the small crated breeds you can very easily attach a small water bowl inside the crate. The type of bowl I am thinking of was, I believe, originally designed to go inside a bird-cage and can be clipped on with two metal prongs. It is unlikely that your dog would be able to upset such a bowl, although if you don't want a wet exhibit you would be wise not to leave the bowl in the crate before your dog goes into the ring, but only after judging is complete.

If you have been 'thrown out' of your class you will presumably wish to stay by the ring-side for a few moments to watch the end of judging and to see which dogs actually win. I can never understand exhibitors who storm out of the ring and hasten back to their benches immediately, none the wiser about which dogs beat their own. I always want to see which dogs won so that I can formulate (in private) my own personal opinion as to whether or not my exhibit was fairly beaten. Of course, one must never lose sight of the fact that the judge's opinion is final and that every judge will have his or her own preferences, added to which the way in which a dog shows himself on the day, his general condition and the way he is handled can also have a bearing on the final placings. Very often one reads a show report in the press saying, 'these three could change places at any time, but . . .'. Such a statement indicates that the judge could fully appreciate that another judge may prefer, for example, the dog placed third to the one placed first but that on the day the winner excelled in, shall we say, 'finish'. Alternatively the writer may understand that another judge might place more emphasis on a different aspect of the anatomy and so reverse the placings.

Everyone knows the saying 'walls have ears'; well, so do ring-sides – many pairs of them in fact! So do be extremely cautious when making comments about other people's exhibits. Only the

judge knows exactly what a dog is like on the day for it is only the
judge who has had the opportunity to go over him. Indeed, even
someone who has judged a particular dog on a previous occasion
does not really know exactly what the dog is like at that show. He
may, for example, be carrying less weight under another judge or
may even have lost a tooth since having been judged by someone
else, and in a youngster many changes may take place between
one show and the next. Do take care, for you will not be highly
thought of if you gossip about a certain dog's supposed faults, and
always remember that the person standing at the side of or behind
you may be a friend or relation of the person whose dog you are
criticising. Just think how hurtful an unkind comment can be and
how you would feel about overhearing such a remark about your
own dog.

Most importantly, please don't spread rumours. Just because
you may have been told that a dog had only five lower incisor
teeth or a crooked front under his heavy coat, don't take that as
the gospel truth unless you have seen for yourself and know the
statement to be a fact. Unfortunately the dog world can be very
cruel and it is certainly not unknown for rumours to spread like
wildfire, stemming only from someone who has a grudge against
another exhibitor or her dog. Try not to get involved in gossip,
and if 'inside information' is disclosed to you, refrain from
comment and turn the other ear until you have proof, for only in
this way will you be fair to all parties concerned. The ring-side
gossipers of the show world soon get to know from whom they get
a response and from whom they do not, so avoid being taken in by
them or you will make yourself more enemies than friends.

If you go to a benched show alone there is always the dilemma
of whether you should be with your dog or watching the judging,
for strictly speaking Kennel Club rules allow a dog to be away
from his bench only for exhibition in his class and for short
periods of exercise. I must leave you to your own judgement in
that regard, but if you do leave your dog on the bench it is always
worthwhile asking a picnicking neighbour to keep a general eye
on him until you return. As mentioned earlier, at Championship
shows you will find that you get to know your neighbours quite
well for dogs are always benched in alphabetical order of the
owners' surnames, and this helps everyone to share the responsibility. If you are away from your dog, do be sure to keep popping
back to look at him frequently and never allow him to be a
nuisance either to other dogs or to people. His benching chain

*Firmly secured by her benching chain which is attached to a leather collar with an identity disc, the author's Deerhound waits perfectly happily. Her very own blanket serves to personalize her bench at every show*

must never be so long that he can get on and off his bench at will, for this is how accidents can happen. Unfortunately one frequently hears announcements over the loudspeakers at shows asking an exhibitor to return immediately to his bench because his dog is in distress.

At shows which are exclusively for dogs, most of the people around the benches are dog people themselves and so would not think of going up to a strange dog or interfering with one. However, especially at shows where there are also other events on the day, such as those combined with an agricultural show, or indeed at Cruft's which is always popular outside the dog world, there are frequently many members of the general public about and these can include unsupervised parties of school children. Show dogs are a constant source of interest to such visitors, many of whom have never owned a dog in their lives and simply do not know how to approach one – and approach they will. So be on your guard against strange fingers poking into your dog's crate or your large dog being woken suddenly from a sound sleep to find a strange little hand on his head. If you have a small dog a coat thrown over the front of the cage is a good deterrent, and some owners of large dogs manage to find something to clip across the front of the bench. One must not obstruct gangways, but a small picnic chair in front of the bench is a good way of putting a certain distance between your dog and enquiring, investigative fingers. As I write this, at a show only yesterday I witnessed one of the groundspeople taunting a dog with a pair of long tweezers he was using to pick up litter from the floor; so I cannot stress enough that you must keep an eye on your dog at all times.

In warm weather it is imperative that your dog receives almost constant attention, for it is surprising how quickly heat can build up, especially in benching tents and other such areas. On especially hot days show societies sometimes make an announcement that due to the extreme heat exhibitors may remove their dogs from the showground before the appointed hour. However, if no such announcement is made you cannot remove your dog from the venue until the time stipulated by the society (if a stipulation is made, as is the case at most of the large Championship shows). Some people like to throw a wet towel over their dogs' backs, but I have reservations about this for I understand that it can have quite the wrong effect and act like a sauna. At the very first sign of heatstroke in a dog you must contact the vet at the show, but it is worth knowing that immersion in cold water is the quickest way of bringing down the body temperature. If your dog is in distress you will usually find knowledgeable people only too willing to help, and don't ever be afraid to ask at the bar or restaurant for an urgent supply of water and ice cubes; such a request has been known to save a dog's life.

When judging of your breed is complete, especially on occasions when yours has been judged first in the ring and you are not yet allowed to leave the venue, you may well find the opportunity to ask others how well or badly they feel you are showing your dog. Get others to watch you move him outside the tent and, between you, you will probably establish the best pace at which he should move. Now is the time to make the most of

*A cold wet day after breed judging is complete is a perfect time to seek words of wisdom from those more experienced than yourself. Here the author (left) warms up with a cup of coffee with her highly respected friend, Mrs Margaret Worth*

conversing with breed experts and to pick up as much constructive information as you can while they have time to spare.

During the lunch break or when showing is over you will undoubtedly want to explore the trade stands. As you go to more and more shows you will get to know which stands are at most shows and which ones are to be found only occasionally, and so you will be able to gauge your supplies. When selecting your dog food, shampoo or conditioner always check that you will be able to get it again when needed. Conditioner and shampoos are most economically purchased in gallon or half-gallon containers, but don't wait until you get right to the bottom before replenishing your supply. Where food is concerned it can be infuriating if you have just got your dog used to a particular food when your stock runs out, the stand-holder who sells it does not attend the next three Championship shows and there is no supplier in your area; so when selecting food check availability as well as content.

# Keeping records

Something I would strongly recommend that you buy at one of your very first shows is a show record book, because you will most definitely need to keep a record of your dog's wins. This will be especially relevant if you are ever lucky enough to have to apply to the Kennel Club for a Junior Warrant, and when you make out your entry for Cruft's you will have to give details of the show, or one of the shows, at which your dog won a place which qualified him for entry. This allows the Kennel Club to check that no dogs without the right to do so are entered for Cruft's. You may also find that the breed club to which you belong has on offer a points trophy. For some such trophies exhibitors have to submit the number of points that their dogs have won at various shows. One I can think of, for example, has the following scoring system for wins at any type of Kennel Club registered show with the exception of Exemption shows.

*Wins in Any Variety classes*

1st place:   4 points
2nd place:   3 points
3rd place:   2 points
4th place:   1 point

*Wins in Breed classes*

1st place:   3 points
2nd place:   2 points
3rd place:   1 point

*Breed Clubs often have trophies on offer for special events and some trophies are allocated on a points system*

Such trophies can be fun to compete for, and with such a scoring system you could pick up just as many points by competing at a local Limited or Sanction show as at major Championship shows. It is indeed very often the novice exhibitors who stand a good chance of winning such trophies because many of the well-established and successful exhibitors in each breed frequently exhibit mainly at Championship show level. You would be surprised to know how few exhibitors actually bother to send in their scores for these trophies – primarily, I believe, because they haven't kept an accurate record. So if you keep your records accurate and constantly up to date, you will already have the edge over many of the other exhibitors.

But don't keep a record only of your dog's wins; you will find it invaluable to keep track of losses too, for usually you will not wish to show your dog under a judge who has thrown him out. However, there can be certain circumstances in which it is well worth giving a dog another try under the same judge. At the show where your dog was unsuccessful he may not have been behaving well on the day, or perhaps he was out of coat or condition, any of which could have prevented him from being placed in the cards. He may also have been up against stiff competition in a large class at a Championship show, whereas under the same judge at a local Open show his chances of being placed would most probably be much greater. For this reason it is helpful to keep a note of why you think he was thrown out, possibly also making a note of the winners of the class (although if you keep your marked-up catalogues neatly filed you will have easy access to that information without making a separate note).

There is a great deal to be said for keeping a good and efficient filing system for your dog, and believe me, it can be a very nostalgic experience to look back on old records when your dog is well past his prime. His triumphs will stay in your memory even more clearly if you have kept details of his career, and nothing can take those away from you.

## Making up your own record book

Making up a record book for your dog can be fairly time-consuming, but if you can spare the time to set it up it will then be easy to complete as time goes on and you will always have all the information you need at your fingertips.

In the first section of your file keep all the general details about your dog: date of birth, name, address and telephone number of breeder, Kennel Club registration number, etc. At the front of your book, be sure to include the address and telephone number of your veterinary surgery, making a note of which vet you prefer to see at the practice. In your dealings with vets you will probably find that you come to have more faith in one than another at your local practice, possibly because he is more used to dealing with dogs, or because he explains things better, or simply because your dog is more comfortable with him than with another. When you book your appointment with the vet don't be afraid to ask specifically if you can see Mr So-and-So, and if your dog is visiting only for a routine injection you can perhaps wait a day until the vet you prefer is available. On the subject of injections, in this section of your record book it will be helpful to keep a full record of any visits to the vet and what they were for. Your dog's vaccination certificate must be kept in a safe place so that it is to hand each time you take him along for a booster, and don't forget that if you have to put your dog in kennels while you are away on holiday a good kennel should ask to see the certificate as proof that your dog's injections are all up to date.

Next you may wish to include your dog's full pedigree with details of his sire and dam and their KC registration and Stud Book Numbers, if applicable, just for reference. Dog shows are, of course, always advertised in the canine press but it is handy to keep a section for forthcoming shows so that any you know about well in advance are not forgotten. It may be that you have thoroughly enjoyed a show one year and have promised yourself that you will make the trip there again. I think each of us has a handful of shows which we consider to be our favourites and which take precedence over others in the show calendar, and you can keep a note of these and details of approximate dates (if exact dates are not yet known) and details of where you can contact the Show Secretaries.

If you have already exhibited at a certain show you will probably find that the society's next schedule is sent to you automatically, but this way you will have the details to hand in case it doesn't pop through the letter-box when you expect it. You may have read in the *Kennel Gazette*, or heard on the proverbial grapevine, that a particular judge will be presiding over your breed in the future; if you have already been reasonably successful under this judge, or have heard, perhaps from your dog's breeder, that she is likely to appreciate your own stock, make a note of this so that you don't overlook the show when the time comes around. It is likely that you will also know well in advance about the dates of shows and other events organised by your breed club, as these are usually included in a newsletter or in the breed note section of the dog press; keep a note of them so that you don't double-book a date in error.

You will be able to keep a separate list of the various shows for which you have actually made your entry, or you can indicate them, perhaps with a large red tick, on the notes you have already made. As well as circling the appropriate classes inside the schedule, I also mark the names of the dogs I have entered on the schedule's cover, together with the date on which I posted the entry form. Such information is always helpful if ever you need to check details of posting in the event that your show passes do not arrive in time. Just a brief reminder here that if ever show day comes around and you have still not received your passes (remembering that they are usually sent out only for Championship shows), take along to the show as much documentary evidence as you can find to prove that you actually did send off the entries – your cheque-book entry is no longer considered sufficient proof but it does help to have it with you to back up your evidence.

Records of your wins can be kept in a separate record book (obtainable from trade stands at most large shows), or you can make a list in your file (providing you are using one of the loose-leaf variety, because otherwise you will run the risk of running rapidly out of space). By designing your own list you can leave as much space as required for making your personal notes about how your dog performed on the day, or why you think the competition beat you, etc. It is also interesting to list the number of entries in your class, for if you have listed a second place its value will have a different significance depending on whether there were twenty-five exhibits in the class or only two. If you wish you can keep two types of listings for your show wins, one giving a detailed account as described above, the other simply giving name and date of show, name of judge, class and place gained; the latter will be useful as a quick and easy reference when totting up points for trophies and warrants and for deciding when your dog is no longer eligible to compete in a certain class.

In the same file you may like also to collect information which can be used in the future. For example, you may have a bitch which, sooner or later, you might decide to mate. When going to shows always keep an eye open for the dogs you like the look of from the ring-side and try to compile their pedigrees so that you can see whether they might suit your bitch if ever you do decide to mate her. Of course, without background knowledge of the dogs incorporated in the pedigree you will need to seek expert advice as to whether your bitch's pedigree will really match up well, but breeding is another subject and cannot be covered in the context of this book. However, if you have started to collect a few pedigrees of the dogs which interest you, you will be well on the way when the time comes, and the very fact that you are bothering to do this will give you a deeper understanding of your breed. When you are trying to compile pedigrees, breeders will usually be of assistance to you, but don't forget that the most useful publication is the Kennel Club's Breed Record Supplement which lists all registered named dogs irrespective of whether they have gained entry into the Stud Book. Often breed clubs give pedigrees of Champions in their newsletters, and for many breeds a book of Champions is available which would be of invaluable assistance to you.

Obviously, if you do eventually end up as a breeder/exhibitor you will be able to incorporate your breeding records in the same file. Similarly, if your show dog is successful enough to become a stud dog you should keep an accurate record of any matings carried out, with details of the bitch, the bitch's owner, the offspring produced, the fee charged and, of course, the date(s) on which mating took place. Just a word of caution on this subject which, again, is not one which can be covered in depth in this book – don't accept stud bookings unless you are sure that the bitch's pedigree is suitable to match up with that of your dog, and don't be tempted to accept just one stud appointment when you know full well that there is very little likelihood of any other bitches coming to your dog. Once your dog has been used at stud there is every chance that you will notice a difference in him: he is likely to be less clean around the house and very possibly more aggressive with other male dogs. It is unfair to allow a dog to be used just once, for when he has mated a bitch he will most probably wish to do so again, and unless your dog is a really top winner, stud enquiries are likely to be few and far between because there are always plenty of Champions and successful proven studs dogs available. Many of these belong to established and successful breeders in their own right, so as a novice exhibitor your own dog will have to be something very special if he is to be in demand.

Perhaps the main thing to remember is that you bought the dog both as a pet and as a potential show specimen. If he is highly successful you will be lucky enough to reap all the rewards that success in the show-ring brings with it, but if he is not one of the dog world's great achievers, don't push him beyond his limits but enjoy the small successes which will, inevitably, come if you try hard, present your dog well and give him all the care and attention he deserves.

# 9
# Making the most of
# your successes

If you have campaigned your dog with a degree of success you probably want to advertise your wins, for it can be to your dog's advantage for people to take notice of him. It is always worth while getting a supply of good photographs of your dog so that these can be incorporated in adverts as and when desired. It is a pity to have a really good win which you would love to advertise with a photo, only to find that you have nothing suitable for use. In such circumstances, by the time you have a photograph taken and developed your big win has probably become history rather than news.

## Photographs

At most shows, certainly the larger ones, you will find one or more professional photographers who specialise in canine photography. You may also be lucky enough to have a semi-professional photographer in your breed who takes some good-quality photos at the shows and is prepared to sell one to you for a small fee; don't be afraid to ask if he will take a photo of your dog, for he will probably be only too pleased to do so. In fairness, though, you must offer to pay, although the fee charged will possibly be lower than if you had gone to one of the top professionals. Having said that, a good photograph is of the utmost importance, so don't be tempted to use an inferior one just because it is cheap.

A photograph used in an advertisement must be clear, of high quality and must do your dog justice. Most advertising media prefer to work from black and white originals (unless of course the advert is to be in colour), but some of them will accept a clear colour photo from which they will make a reproduction in black and white. The latter rarely gives quite such good results as does a black and white original, and you must be sure that there is plenty of contrast between the background and the dog. It is no good, for example, having a dark dog standing in front of a dark green bush – while it may look acceptable in colour, in black and white the dog will simply be lost. Try also to avoid too much clutter in the picture; many people who submit their own photos tend to have the dog in front of the fireplace, standing on a highly patterned carpet and perhaps with a few trophies behind him. Such a photo will do absolutely nothing for your image, nor for that of your dog. You want to show the rest of the dog-showing world the merits of your *dog*, not your sitting-room carpet!

Try to choose a photograph which shows your dog in good condition and coat, and one which does justice to his balance. I think some of the worst photos are those taken of a small dog which is perched on an even smaller table so that his back legs are tucked in behind him, making him look all bunched up and possibly also high on the back-end. Stand your dog for the photographer just as you would for the judge in the ring and you can't go far wrong.

Not all photographs, however, have to be of a dog in show pose. You may prefer a head study or a sitting posture, or you may even like to include yourself in the photo to help to get your own face better known. After all, it is you who are paying for the advertisement so it is your prerogative to choose what you want. All I would say is that if you haven't got a good photo you would probably be better advised not to use one at all. Incidentally, if you have a black dog you will have to be even more careful than usual when selecting the photo, for it is only too easy to have a long-haired black dog ending up looking like a black blob when it gets into print; at least if your dog is black and short-coated you should be able to see a clear outline.

Photographs are sometimes returned (depending on where you advertise), so be sure to mark 'Please return to . . .' on the back of the picture and, whatever you do, print the dog's name clearly on the back for you would, I'm sure, be very disappointed if your own dog's photo were to be printed alongside someone else's advert. What I am saying may sound rather basic advice but it is quite surprising what people do; before now I've had photographs sent to me with no description at all and I've had to work out which dog is which from the post-office frank on the envelope. The other thing you really must remember is not to breach copyright. All professional photographers will give clear instructions with the photographs they provide and you may or may not have to pay a small fee to use the photo in an advert, usually depending upon the publication. As a matter of courtesy it is, however, always polite to give the name of the photographer in your advertisement whether or not he has specified that this must be done; usually this is included in small print immediately underneath the photo or it can be written vertically along the side so as not to detract from the advertisement content below.

## Content of advertisement

When preparing your advertisement, lay it out as clearly as you can for if it is at all misleading you cannot hold the printer responsible for having made an error. It should ideally be typewritten, but if not you must print the text very clearly. Always keep in mind that although you may be perfectly familiar with the spelling of your dog's name, it will probably be totally strange to the person responsible for compiling the advert at the other end, and spellings of names cannot be checked in a dictionary. Try to make it clear, too, which words or lines need emphasis. Usually you will want the name of your dog to stand out most prominently, but if you are advertising in a breed club magazine and you have your own affix you may want the affix to stand out predominantly at the head of the page. If you decide to give the name of the sire and dam of your dog under his name, this is usually put in smaller print and is frequently in brackets. To save space you need not write 'sire' and 'dam' but you can put 'x' or 'ex' between the two names, and always remember that the sire's name comes before that of the dam.

The content and layout of the advertisement will inevitably vary according to the type of publication and whether you are advertising a particular win or simply placing the advert to get the name of your dog better known. Again I would advise you to avoid clutter. It is often useful to give the names of the sire and dam, especially if your dog is, as yet, little known, but this is not essential if you wish to save space. Advertisements generally give the name of the owner and usually also the address or telephone number at the foot of the advertisement. Any additional information is, naturally, of your choosing. You may like to boast about a certain win or number of wins, but if all you have to boast about at this stage is a fourth or fifth place in, for example, an Any Variety class at an Open show you would be best advised not to mention it. Of course you should be justly proud of your dog's placing, but you will run the risk of it being totally overshadowed by someone else's advertisement announcing a Best in Show win or a Junior Warrant achievement. Instead you can use a sentence such as 'I would like to thank the judges for Fred's consistent placings at Open shows this year' or similar wording. Some people insist on giving a long list of various placings which, unless they represent very substantial achievements, do nothing more than indicate that the advertiser is a novice who has not yet met with any top-level successes.

But please don't let my comments deter you from placing adverts, for they are certainly a good way of getting your name known, especially within your own breed, and you will always be able to save a copy of the publication in your scrapbook. Of course, if you have a really big win then you can tell everyone about it with great pride. A first prize at Championship level (especially in an age class or one of the higher classes) or Best of Breed or better at Open show level are well worth publicising. If your new puppy is constantly in the cards you can describe him as a 'consistent prize-winner', or if he has won, say, two firsts, a second and a third at his first four shows the listing of these wins makes logical sense for it is telling the reader that he has not yet been thrown out; effectively this means a lot.

If you do decide to use a photograph in your advert make sure that you allow sufficient space; it is no good cramming a photo and a lot of wordage into the minimum space allowable, for the effect will be lost. Usually for a moderate extra fee it is possible to have more than one photograph included, but remember that if you do this each picture will be proportionately a lot smaller, so be careful that the impact is not lost. When submitting more than one photo take extra care that the printer will understand fully which caption belongs to which photograph. Colour advertisements cost a lot more than black and white but can certainly give added impact, although not all media offer colour advertising and if they do they generally specify the minimum size of the advert which is usually quite large.

One very important fact which you must remember is that you

must never make false claims in an advert or you could land yourself in trouble. Never lay claim to something you haven't done, or over-exaggerate your dog's wins. A typical mistake made by many is found in adverts stating that 'show quality' puppies are for sale, often at the age of eight or twelve weeks. It is simply not possible to know whether such a young puppy will turn out to be worthy of entry at shows, and such advertisers could find themselves accused of having contravened the Trade Descriptions Act, so don't fall into that trap, or a similar one, yourself.

## Where to advertise

If you are aiming simply to publicise your dog's wins or to get your own or your dog's name better known, the canine newspapers are always a good place to advertise, for the readership is high; this is a particularly good medium for wins of topical interest such as any recent important achievement. The most usual place for such an advert is in the breed note section, so make sure the breed of your dog is clearly stated in your correspondence. You know that your Lhasa Apso is an Apso, but does the young lady who is laying out the copy for that issue of the newspaper? Just occasionally one finds an Apso featured under the Shih Tzu breed notes, to cite just two breeds as an example. Always remember to state the exact size of your advert and to enclose the appropriate cheque or postal order; you will find full details of the cost per single column centimetre towards the back of the papers.

Publishers of the canine weeklies produce special issues and features from time to time. If they are planning to cover your breed you will, if you enter Championship shows and therefore have your name and address listed in the catalogue, probably be approached by them asking if you wish to take advertising space. This, certainly, would be a publication read by many enthusiasts of your chosen breed and may well be kept by people for reference, so you should certainly not dismiss the idea of placing a general advert. Sometimes the papers do special features on certain shows, so if you have had a good win at the show you may choose to advertise with a photograph which can be taken by the photographer in attendance at the show. Other special issues come out for Junior Warrant winners and for Cruft's; in the former you must, of course, already have done a substantial amount of winning to have obtained your dog's warrant, but usually anyone can advertise in the Cruft's special supplements if they wish, although naturally you will be most interested in doing this if your dog has qualified for this special show.

Both *Our Dogs* and *Dog World* publish yearly annuals. These come out just before Christmas and are packed with several hundred pages of adverts relating to all breeds. In addition there are a few articles, usually by regular contributors to the canine press, so they are very popular with most show-goers and can usually be found on the shelves of major newsagencies around Christmas time. There is really little point in advertising a list of your dog's wins in such a publication for this information is likely to mean little to readers of these annuals. You would do better to restrict yourself to just a couple of lines with your name, address, telephone number and kennel name if you have one. Several of the eminent breeders in most breeds spend hundreds of pounds advertising in the canine annuals, sometimes taking several full pages, occasionally in colour. I suspect that it is the well-established breeders and exhibitors who benefit most from advertising in this medium and unless you have limitless money to spend on advertising, I think as a novice you would be wiser to spend your money in the weekly canine press or in breed club magazines, which we shall come to in a moment. However, if you do decide to advertise in the annuals you can usually save yourself a little money by booking early, as often a discount is offered to those who send in their copy and pre-payment well before the closing date; details of advertisement charges and any discounts available are generally published via the weekly dog papers in the latter half of the preceding year.

Before we do discuss breed club publications, let us not forget the few monthly journals which exist. Those which are regularly to be found on the newsagent's shelf are aimed primarily at the pet market, and advertisers are therefore more likely to find benefit in advertising puppies for sale rather than publicising a show dog's wins. The *Kennel Gazette* is the other monthly. A high proportion of its readers are show people, but this is not a magazine which carries the type of advertisements about which we are speaking.

Let us move on to breed club publications, which are of great value to the novice and seasoned exhibitor alike. Most of the larger breed clubs publish a booklet, or at least a newsletter, one or more times each year. Providing that the club has a healthy list of members, advertising in such a magazine will help you to reach just the people you need, so that they can get to know you and your dog better. Kennel Club registered breed clubs are not profit-making organisations and so the cost of advertising is usually kept to a minimum. Most clubs work on the principle that if the sum collected per page is just a little more than the actual production cost of one page then that money goes towards the cost of printing the 'news' pages of the booklet, so keeping the publication economically viable. As a result, in placing such adverts you are not only helping yourself and your dog but also the breed club to which you belong. In such a publication you can place as much relevant information as you wish, for the readers will all be people involved with your own specific breed and so the entire readership should be interested in what you have to say. Nevertheless, I would still suggest that you avoid clutter. In my mind a simple bold advert stands out much better than a page packed full of so much information that many people either don't bother to read it all or cannot understand exactly what message the advertiser is trying to put across.

When deciding what is topical and what is not you should also bear in mind that, especially in the case of booklets incorporating photographic advertisements, the closing date for booking your advert will probably be several weeks before the publication is circulated to members, to allow sufficient time for printing. You should also remember that most people keep their booklets for several years and that they are frequently used for reference purposes.

## Contribution to breed club newsletters

Newsletter editors are often glad to have interesting short articles for inclusion in their club's publications. Obviously, whether or not an article is considered suitable for publication rests with the editors but there is absolutely no harm in you, as a novice exhibitor, sending in an interesting little story which, if included, will help to get your name known by other members of the club. Many editors like to have a good cross-section of material which will be of interest to seasoned exhibitors, newcomers to the breed and members who perhaps simply have one much-loved pet. In such an article it would be inappropriate to try to boast about your dog's wins for that would probably be turned down, being considered free advertising. You could, however, write about how you have been bitten by the show bug or how much pleasure you are deriving from your new-found companion, for example. If the first article you submit is not accepted, don't be too despondent; try a story with a different angle another time and you should soon see your name in print.

## Breed note writers

Both of the canine weekly papers have one or more breed note correspondents who write up the columns of news for their specific breed, and they are always on the lookout for snippets of interesting information which other readers would like to hear about, so do contact them to tell them about any really big win you have. They will not, of course, be able to include the various less prestigious prizes you have won, for if they did so the breed columns would be cluttered with information which can, in any event, be read in the judges' critiques in another section of the paper. But if you have had a Best in Show, Reserve Best in Show or Best Puppy in Show win this will usually readily be included in the column. Sometimes it is possible to get a mention for a Best of Breed or Best Puppy in Breed win, but do bear in mind that even if a breed note writer submits this information to a paper the editors may decided to cut it due to a shortage of space or the fact that they do not think it worthy of inclusion. Nevertheless, don't be embarrassed to contact the appropriate person about your win – the worst they can say is, 'No, I can't fit it in' and at best you may get a little bit of free publicity, which can't be a bad thing. You will find the names of the breed correspondents by looking at the foot of the appropriate column in the canine press, and the *Our Dogs* annual actually includes a list of correspondents with their address and telephone numbers. If you cannot locate your breed correspondent, perhaps through a breed club list of members or a show catalogue, you may send a letter to the relevant newspaper for that person's attention; this, though, is not the fastest way of getting your news into print so try to contact the person directly if you possibly can.

# Moving up the classes

If your dog has won well you will automatically have won your way out of the lower classes and will therefore now have to compete in the higher ones in which the competition is much stiffer. There are, in fact, certain cases in which having had a great deal of success with a dog can make showing difficult later on. If, for example, a judge has awarded a Challenge Certificate to a dog in one of the Puppy classes or in Junior, that dog is then ineligible for any other class below Limit unless he is still of an age to enter one of the classes restricted to age. But as Special Yearling classes are few and far between, this often means that at the age of eighteen months and one day he has to be entered in Limit, a very strong class indeed. In certain breeds this is not unusual but in others it means that the dog is up against much more mature dogs when he himself is probably at that awkward change-of-coat stage. Faced with this dilemma you must seriously ask yourself whether you should perhaps retire your exhibit from the ring for a few months until he is sufficiently mature to hold his own in such a class. If you do decide to continue campaigning him in Limit you run the risk of being 'knocked', and this will not do his reputation any good at all.

We have already touched on the fact that different breeds appear to have different feelings about what is and what is not considered acceptable with regard to jumping classes. Whatever the general feeling within your own breed, in a book such as this, which is endeavouring to give you tips which will help you do well with your dog, I think it only fair to say that there are cases in which you will perhaps stand a greater chance of success if you jump the odd class.

Just suppose that you thoroughly enjoy showing your dog but have never won a first prize. Suppose also that your dog is one of the long-coated breeds and is now a few years old, in full bloom and looking much more mature than the rest of the dogs in the Maiden and Novice classes in which, technically, he can still be entered. A judge looking at your dog in a class such as these will immediately ask herself why such a mature and glamorous-looking dog is still in such a low class. 'There must be something wrong,' she will say to herself. And so your dog has an obstacle to overcome even before the judge has laid hands on him. This being the case, you would be wiser to move him up to Post Graduate (or at a breed club show with a large number of classes you may be better advised to try Tyro or Under Graduate), a class in which both the judge and the ring-siders can be allowed to think that he had done at least a bit of winning. Let's face it, nobody wants their dog to stay in Novice for ever! Equally, if you introduce your dog to the show-ring for the first time as a mature dog it is not really sensible to go into Maiden or Novice, even though the reason for lack of winning may be perfectly legitimate in that he has never been shown. In fact, you will often find that a breeder decides to show a bitch after she has raised one or two litters, and in most cases it is quite accepted that she is entered straight into the Post Graduate or even Limit class.

# Retiring your dog

Unfortunately not every 'hopeful' is destined for a successful show career, and sooner or later you may reach the unhappy conclusion that it is time to call it a day. If you genuinely believe that you are showing your dog to his best advantage but still you are not getting placed, either under all-rounders or under breed specialists, then perhaps you should retire him from the ring. Of course, you can continue to show just for the fun of it if you wish, but it is an expensive hobby and I think that sooner or later you will find it rather frustrating to keep exhibiting a dog which doesn't win.

Even if you retire your dog from the show-ring proper you can still take him around to Exemption shows, and even other very small ones; that way you will still keep up social contact with fellow exhibitors and get a lot of pleasure out of such occasions. Probably a harder-hearted breeder or exhibitor than I would advise you to find a good pet home for your dog and immediately to look around for a replacement. While I thoroughly agree that if you enjoy showing and want to carry on with the hobby seriously you should certainly make headway with regard to getting another dog to show, I find it exceedingly hard to part with those dogs of my own which I have retired from the ring for various reasons. As a result, I have a large number of 'passengers'. Just because a bitch may have knocked out a tooth, I can't love her any the less, and so I am soft enough to hang on to most of my oldies. Indeed, I feel that if you and your dog really enjoy each other's company it is your duty to keep him with you if you possibly can. However, if it is really necessary to part with your not so successful show dog in order to make room for another one, you really must choose his new home very carefully. Locally based relations are often useful in such circumstances for it is possible that the dog may already have visited the home in question and will therefore be familiar with the family members and the new territory. Alternatively, you may have an old friend whom you trust implicitly and with whom you feel sure your dog will be happy. If the dog stays in your local vicinity you will be able to monitor his progress and perhaps give a little help and advice when necessary. In any event, you must be prepared to take him back if things don't work out well. Always remember that when you took on your young puppy you did so with a view to keeping him for the rest of his life. It's not his fault that his front went a bit crooked or he grew a touch larger than required for the breed, so do make sure that his non-showing days are just as enjoyable for him as his show days were.

## Unsuccessful stock

However good or bad the quality of your own dog, you must at all times keep the good of the breed in mind. If, sadly, your first show bitch turned out not to be a winner, please don't be tempted to breed from her if she has faults which cannot be overlooked. Only the very best-quality stock should be used in breeding pro-grammes. Certainly, a bitch which is sound and typical but not up to top winning may well be valuable in a breeding programme and prove to be a worthwhile brood, but don't be tempted to use anything for breeding purposes which has very serious faults. And this goes for dogs as well as bitches. In any breed there will usually be plenty of high-quality stud dogs available, so there is no need to make use of inferior stock.

I do not say this to be hard but for the good of your breed and for your own good, too. So many times one sees novice exhibitors set off along the show road, meet with almost total failure, and end up breeding from the very dog that was not a success in the ring in the hope of breeding a 'good one' of their own. Like does not always beget like, but if you eventually decide that you want to breed you really must start by breeding from high-quality stock or your breeding programme will either completely flop or will take very many years to achieve a level at which you can produce consistent winners. There is always the possibility that there will be one good puppy in a litter, and many are tempted to take the risk that they will get just that one who will prove to be a winner. But in breeding one must think in the long term and must therefore consider that that winning puppy and its litter-mates are likely to reproduce the poorer qualities of their sire or dam. What you must be looking for are good qualities in every generation so that you can go on to produce better and better stock. Planning in this way will help you to meet with long-term success, not just one flier (if you are very lucky) which is unable to reproduce his or her kind. When breeding, the litters which are looked upon by established breeders as the most successful are those in which all the litter is both sound and typical – what is known as an 'even litter'. Unless you use the right breeding stock, even litters are notoriously hard to produce.

## Breeding from a successful bitch

Let us now look on the more positive side. Suppose you have been campaigning a bitch and she has won well, perhaps having gained first, second or third prizes at Championship level on a fairly consistent basis. Clearly you have been bitten by the show bug, but you would also like to have a litter from your bitch for two reasons: a) she is of such a high quality that you feel her offspring are likely to be a credit to the breed, and b) you would like to keep a puppy of your own breeding to show. I cite these as the two main reasons for wishing to breed, for if these two factors are not applicable then you really have no reason to breed. Obviously there are many more considerations than these, such as whether you have the time and resources to raise a litter and whether you feel certain that you have sufficient suitable prospective homes for the puppies. This is a vast subject which I cannot go into in depth here but I would strongly advise you to read all the relevant material you can before making the very serious decision that you want to breed. Something you must most certainly *not* do is make a decision to breed in the hope that you will make a profit from breeding, for that is quite the wrong attitude. In any case, if you set yourself up correctly so that your bitch and puppies are housed, equipped and fed as they should be then your first litter will probably be quite a costly affair, especially if you are unlucky enough also to be faced with heavy veterinary bills.

But let us assume that you have looked into the subject very thoroughly and still feel that you would like to have a litter from your bitch. You will, of course, be faced with the dilemma of when you should breed from her as this will mean that she cannot be shown for a while. Much will depend upon the breed in question, so you must seek the advice of prominent people within your breed as to the best age for a bitch to whelp her first litter. In general, and I must stress that this is not specific to any particular breed, in the smaller breeds it is not recommended that a bitch produces a litter before the age of eighteen months, and with the larger breeds two is considered a better minimum age although some breeders are happier if bitches are a little older. Under no circumstances should a bitch be mated prior to her second season. As a very general rule it is thought wisest if a bitch is allowed to have her first litter by the time she is about four years old.

So, if your bitch is winning well it is, in theory, possible to keep her in the ring up to the age of four and then to mate her to the dog of your choice, which will give her a good while in the show-ring before her litter. However, it may be sensible to bear in mind that there is always the possibility that you won't get a mating at the planned season, or that after her mating she does not produce puppies, in which case you would have to wait another six months at least and so you could be running the risk of her going beyond the optimum maximum age for producing a first litter. With this in mind, and also giving due consideration to the fact that bitches in some breeds are more difficult to get into whelp than others, you would perhaps be wiser to consider trying to mate her by the age of three.

The other thing you will need to consider carefully is how long she will be out of the ring following her mating. It is not really wise to show a bitch soon after she has been mated, for even though in the first few weeks she will not be showing signs of her litter, you would be exposing her unnecessarily to infection. She will carry her litter for about nine weeks and will then usually spend at least eight weeks in the company of her pups. Granted, you will probably have weaned them by the sixth or seventh week, but I feel it a little unfair suddenly to deprive the dam of her litter as soon as it is weaned, and certainly my own bitches get a great deal of pleasure from their puppies until they are ready to leave home. Having said that, I know that some exhibitors, if they are anxious to get a bitch back into show condition, insist that she leaves her puppies as soon as they are weaned. But that is for you to decide.

Following a litter it can take a bitch several months to get back into the peak of condition physically, and if you have a long-coated breed you must expect her to be out of the ring for anything up to a year, or even longer, depending upon how quickly the coat grows. Some owners of long-coated breeds find it best to clip the coat short as soon as they know the bitch is in whelp, for in this way at least when the coat does grow in again it grows evenly all over. If you try to keep the bitch in long coat you can be disappointed to find, for example, that the body coat begins to look lovely but that her back legs are still almost bare and this, believe me, is most frustrating. Don't, however, clip the coat down until you are absolutely certain she is having a litter (I usually leave it until about the seventh week in whelp) for it would be very sad if she reabsorbed her pups (yes, this can happen in some bitches) or was having a false pregnancy, in which case you would have no puppies and no show dog either.

Don't be tempted to take her back into the ring until she is really looking good again. It's no good explaining to the judge that she's just had a litter; what the judge is interested in is how the dog looks on the day, not how she would look if she hadn't had a litter. If you take her in too soon you will be sorry you did, for you will probably be disappointed with your placings, and you will also want her to retain the good reputation she had achieved before you took her out of the ring to bring up a litter.

Something you simply must do is keep involved with the breed, even though you may not have a dog to show for a while. If you have won well with your bitch in her first couple of years in the ring, your face will have begun to be familiar to others in the breed; stay away from the ring-side and breed events for several months or a year and you will be surprised how quickly your face is forgotten. So keep going to shows, albeit simply as an onlooker, and who knows, you may even be lucky enough to be asked to handle someone else's dog for them if, for example, they have two dogs through to the challenge for Best of Sex. Even just a few moments in the ring will help to keep you in the limelight. Of course, all of us who show say that people don't, or at least shouldn't, 'face judge', but in reality there are always a few who do. In a case where a judge is splitting hairs between two dogs there is always the chance that she will give the higher placing to the dog belonging to the face she recognises. We would all like to live in a perfect world, but unfortunately the human world is not perfect and neither is the world of show dogs, so make sure you give yourself and your dog every possible advantage – and it may help if you are recognised as an exhibitor who has a sincere interest in the breed.

## Showing more than one dog

Of course, there is always the possibility that you have so thoroughly enjoyed showing your first dog that you decide to buy a second. If you have decided to breed from your first bitch then getting another will make matters much easier from a show point of view, for you will have something to take in the ring while she raises her litter. One word of caution here, though: do make sure that if you are going to shows while you have a litter at home you do not let the dog which has been shown come into contact with the puppies before they are fully inoculated. Also be sure to wash your hands thoroughly before you go into the puppies' quarters, and if you are to take real precautions you ought not to wear your show clothes and show shoes in the puppies' immediate environment. I know it can be a chore to have to wash and change before you go in to check your puppies, but if you really care about them you will do just this for you will not wish to expose them to infection any more than necessary. Something else you will have to consider is how long the puppies can safely be left while you go to a show. With any luck there will be a non-showing (but capable) member of the family who can keep an eye on things while you are away, but if not you will have to restrict the time you spend away from home. Only you can decide how long you can, with clear conscience, leave your bitch and puppies alone, but it should be pointed out that a bitch can go from the very first visible stage of pyometra to total collapse and death within seven hours. It is to be hoped that you will not have a bitch which develops pyometra, but you should be aware that this is something which can and does happen, so if you don't have anyone to look after your bitch and her litter while you are at a show you would be wise to go only to those which are within reasonable travelling distance and to get away as soon as possible after judging. If there are two of you who normally go to shows together if would be practical if one of you were to stay at home, for you must also remember that a litter of puppies will need to be fed at regular intervals when they are no longer fully dependent upon the bitch.

Of course, by the time you buy your second show dog you will be a little wiser than you were when you bought your first and, having been involved with the breed for a while, you will have done your homework and bought wisely without falling into too many traps. You may, for whatever reason, not wish to breed from your bitch and I hope I have already made it clear that breeding is not something I recommend unless the circumstances are exactly right; this being the case, you will now have two dogs to campaign at the same time. Naturally it costs more to campaign two dogs than one (though not twice as much, for you only have to fill one car with petrol, park one car, buy one catalogue and, for that matter, take one picnic). But there are other considerations to be made. Is your car suitable to accommodate two dogs? Will you need to invest in partitioning for the back of your estate car in case the dogs don't travel easily together? Will you manage to cope with two dogs at a show if you travel alone, and will you be able to do justice to both in the show-ring?

Presumably your dogs are at least a few months apart in age, and if you have one of each sex you will not usually find that classes clash except at Open and Limited shows where there is often not a separate classification for each sex or at shows with a very high entry where there is one judge for dogs and another for bitches, both sexes occasionally being judged at the same time. In some of the less popular breeds the classes are for mixed sexes even at Championship level, but these are the exception rather than the rule. So if you have two of the same sex, two of similar age, or if you enter at a show which does not have a wide classification, you could find yourself in difficulty in that both dogs are eligible for the same class but you have only one pair of hands. However, there may be two of you going to the show and if, say, there is no Minor Puppy class available and your own dogs are seven months and eleven months, you may feel that your only option is to enter them in the same class. Think carefully before you do so. Of course, if you have someone to handle your other dog you may enter them both in the same class if you wish, but there is, after all, only one first prize so you may like to consider entering one in a different class.

There are two ways of looking at this. Normally, if one of the two dogs is, or looks, more mature than the other it is he whom you should place in the higher class, but in the case of youngsters you may feel that if your eleven-month-old has a chance of winning the class you would be wiser to leave him in the Puppy class and move the baby into a Maiden class if available. Clearly your young puppy would look entirely out of place in one of the more senior classes, so if no Maiden or Novice class is available you would be unwise to choose this option. On the other hand, if you feel your young puppy is still in with a chance in the Puppy class (remembering that the competition in Puppy is usually stronger than Maiden) then you may decide to risk putting your eleven-month-old dog in Junior or one of the other classes. In the case of older dogs when, for example, neither has won his way out of Novice it would be sensible to put the more mature-looking of the two in the next class up.

If ever you have the opportunity to do so you would be well advised not to enter your two show dogs in consecutive classes but to leave a class in between. This is more important in a breed which requires a lot of grooming, for if you have to rush out of one class and into the next you will not have the opportunity to get him looking his very best. With a short-coated dog it is a little easier, but at a benched show the benches, unfortunately, are not always close to the ring so you may have to make a mad dash to the bench and back again unless you have someone who will have your dog standing by in the wings.

Sometimes, of course, consecutive classes are unavoidable and if you do have different dogs in two such classes you really must be well prepared, because although a steward will usually hold up judging for a very short while if you explain the situation, you will rarely be allowed more than a couple of extra minutes for this is not entirely fair on either the judge or the other exhibitors. If you get thrown out in your first class you may just about scrape in on time for you will have those few extra minutes while the judge makes her final placing and makes notes. But if you are lucky enough to be first or even second, the judge will probably want to make notes on your dog so you will be obliged to remain in the ring until the very end of the class; the next class may even be assembling in the ring while the notes are being taken, so you will be cutting things very fine indeed. As I said, such a situation cannot always be avoided but do try to avoid it if you can, and if you can't make sure you are as well prepared as possible – not forgetting to change your ring number, of course.

# 10

# Helpful extras

Canine terminology can be very confusing to the newcomer and is further complicated by the fact that certain features, colours in particular, are described by different names according to the breed. Added to this there is a certain parlance among show-goers which comes as a shock to the novice. One frequently meets with a look of horror when announcing that a dog has been 'thrown out'. 'Good gracious, whatever for?' is the most usual reply, the person to whom one is imparting this information clearly not referring to the fact that the quality of the dog is such that he would not expect it to be thrown out, but that the dog must have done some dreadful misdeed in order to have been thus punished!

To the non-show-going person the term 'Very Highly Commended' often sounds impressive. Indeed, it is often clear that the listener is much more impressed by that than by the proud announcement that a dog has been awarded a Reserve Challenge Certificate which, without explanation, means absolutely nothing to the uninitiated. Many a newcomer gives a false impression to non-doggy friends by boasting about his dog's several Very Highly Commended awards; to the show-goer, someone who needs to publicise these is clearly in short supply of the red and blue cards (and the big green ones) which are indicative of much greater success.

In reading the preceding chapters you will probably already have become familiar with some of the terminology used, but I think it may be helpful for me to include here a couple of glossaries, one giving actual canine terminology in its most general sense, the other listing some of the words and expressions which you are likely to come across when talking to doggy people. Although the first appears fairly extensive it certainly does not cover all of the terms you are likely to encounter, many of which will be specific to your own particular breed. I have, however, included as many as possible of the terms in fairly frequent use. These should play some part in helping you not only to understand what people are saying to you about your dog but also to make more sense of some of the judging critiques which you will find in the canine press.

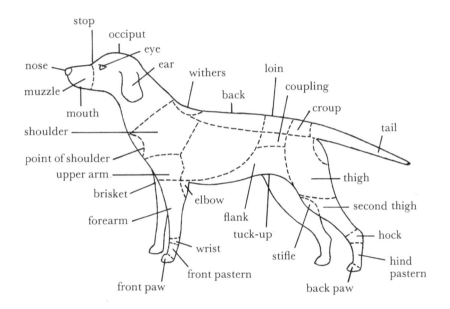

# Canine terms

*Action*   The gait or movement of a dog.

*Affix*   A name granted to breeders by the Kennel Club upon payment of a fee. Sometimes also referred to as a prefix.

*Anal glands*   Two small glands located one on each side of the rectum, just inside the rim of the anal sphincter and functioning as storage chambers for a secretion.

*Angulation*   A term used with reference to the various angles made by bones meeting at different joints. The term 'well angulated' is used in relation to a dog's correctness of angulation for its particular breed. The degree of angulation required on a German Shepherd, for example, is considerably greater than that required for a Chow.

*Ankle joint*  A human anatomical term sometimes used instead of hock joint.

*Apish*  Having a monkey-like expression.

*Apple-headed*  Having a skull which is rounded, as in the King Charles Spaniel and Chihuahua.

*Balance*  A pleasing and well-proportioned blend of a dog's various features resulting in harmonious symmetry.

*Barrel ribs*  Ribs beginning to arch outwards as soon as they leave the vertebral column, thus giving a barrel shape to the chest. A fault in many breeds but in others a character of the breed, as in the Bulldog and Shih Tzu.

*Beard*  Profuse whiskers, often of a somewhat wiry texture, as in the Wire-Haired Dachshund and Afghan Hound.

*Bite*  The position of the upper and lower teeth in relation to each other when the mouth is closed.

*Blaze*  A white marking located on the centre line of the face or forehead.

*Bloom*  Glossy, lustrous coat.

*Blue*  Colour used for a dog which is blue-grey in appearance. This is in fact a dilution of a black coat colour. It is a fault in some breeds but perfectly acceptable in others, the Bedlington Terrier and Kerry Blue Terrier being prime examples.

*Bobtail*  A tail which has been docked to a very short length or a dog which was actually born without a tail. (Also a commonly used term for an Old English Sheepdog.)

*Bone*  Used in connection with substance of bone and frequently with particular reference to the bones of the fore-hand construction.

*Brace*  Two dogs of the same breed.

*Breeching*  Tan-coloured hair on the thighs of certain breeds of short-coated dogs, or the fringing of longish hair in the same area of others. In some short-coated breeds it also refers to the pattern of slightly longer hair in the thigh region. Other words used for these features are trousers or culottes.

*Breed characteristics*  Those features of a breed which distinguish a dog as being typical of its breed.

*Breeder/Br.*  The owner of the bitch at the time of whelping, or the person to whom the bitch was leased for the purpose, the latter having been officially arranged with the Kennel Club. (The breeder is therefore not necessarily the person who actually whelps the litter.)

*Brindle*   A colour pattern giving an almost striped effect due to a mixture of light and dark hair. The background or main colour is usually tan, brown, yellow or grey.

*Brisket*   The lower part of the body which is in front of the chest and between the fore legs.

*Broken coat*   A term used to describe crinkly, harsh and wiry coats such as is to be found on the Wire Fox Terrier for example.

*Broken colour*   A coat pattern in which the main colour is broken up by another colour, usually white.

*Brood bitch*   One kept primarily for breeding purposes, often after her show career is over.

*Brush*   A tail which is heavy with hair and bushy, like that of a fox.

*Butterfly nose*   A nose in which the black pigment is broken by spots of flesh colour.

*Button ear*   One which drops over in front, such as that of the Fox Terrier.

*Canines*   The canine teeth are the four large 'fang' teeth located at the outer edge of each row of incisors. They are the longest and strongest teeth in a dog's mouth.

*Cape*   The profuse hair, often of a harsher texture, which lies around the region of the shoulder in some breeds. Also frequently called a shawl.

*Cat foot*   A round, compact foot with well-arched toes. The pads of the toes should be thick.

*Challenge Certificate/CC*   A Kennel Club award for the best exhibit of one sex at a Championship show, indicating that the exhibit to which it is awarded has challenged all comers. (Challenge Certificates are not automatically available for every breed at every show.)

*Champion/Ch.*   Any Hound, Terrier, Utility, Working (except Border Collie) or Toy dog which has won three Challenge Certificates under three different judges, at least one of the CCs having been awarded after the age of twelve months. Also, any Gundog which has been awarded three CCs as outlined above and has won either a) a Prize, Award of Honour, Diploma of Merit or Certificate of Merit under the Regulations of the Kennel Club or Irish Kennel Club, or b) a Show Gundog Working Certificate which conforms to the conditions set out in the KC Regulations or the Rules of the Irish Kennel Club. (See also Show Champion.)

*Championship show* One at which the Kennel Club grants Challenge Certificates to be awarded.

*Chest* That section of the body between the brisket and the belly (not the front part of the body).

*China eye* A blue wall eye. (See Wall eye.)

*Chiselling* Clean-cut lines and contours, especially on the head and foreface.

*Clean neck* Tight fitting skin around the neck with no wrinkles, loose skin or dewlap. Also known as a dry neck.

*Cloddy* Denoting a thick, heavy-set build.

*Cobby* Of compact conformation. Rather short in the back and well ribbed up. The term relates to the overall body shape.

*Comb* The fine fringe of hair which hangs from the tail of a Setter.

*Commended* The seventh place in a class. (Rarely on offer except at breed club (Championship shows or sometimes in Stakes classes which command a very high entry.)

*Compact* The union of various parts of the body being firmly joined together.

*Condition* A dog said to be in good condition is one which is in a state of suitable physical fitness for the purpose required; that is to say that the points essential for the dog's purpose in life (be it show or work) are well developed.

*Conformation* The various parts of the body assembled together to make a balanced whole. A dog typical of its breed is said to conform to breed type or to have good conformation.

*Congenital* Describing a feature (usually with reference to a defect) which is present at birth, as opposed to one which develops at a later stage in a dog's life.

*Couple* Two hounds.

*Coupling* That part of the body of the dog which joins the forequarters to the hindquarters. One often hears of a dog being short coupled, which means that the area between the last rib and the start of the hindquarter section is relatively short and therefore strong. Long or loose coupling denotes length in this area, often a structural weakness.

*Cow hocked* Having legs resembling those of a cow with the hocks turning inwards. Such construction tends to make the hind pasterns brush together resulting in a lack of freedom of movement.

*Crabbing* Movement like that of a crab. The hind feet move out of parallel with the fore feet.

*Crest*    The top part of the arch in a dog's neck. Used especially in relation to some of the sporting breeds. Crest can also denote the tuft of long sparse hair on the top of the head of the Chinese Crested.

*Critiques*    Reports written by judges following their appointment to judge. Usually the canine press print critiques of first and second prize-winners at Championship shows (and some breed club Open shows) and of the first prize-winners at shows of other levels. The names of owners and dogs having won first, second and third prizes in each class are also usually included in the critique.

*Cropped ears*    The practice of cutting the ears to make them stand erect. Still permissible in some breeds abroad but banned in England since 1895.

*Croup*    The muscular area above and around the area of tail set.

*Cryptorchid*    A male dog in which either one or both of the testicles have not descended into the scrotum. A dog with one undescended testicle is a unilateral cryptorchid (see also monorchid, for the two are frequently confused). When neither testicle is descended the term used is bilateral cryptorchid.

*Cushion*    The thick part of the upper lip in dogs such as the Mastiff, giving the impression of fullness.

*Cushioning*    The thick padding on the upper lip or flews. Also used in connection with the cheek area of some breeds.

*Dewlap*    The pendulous loose skin under a dog's throat, as in the Bloodhound.

*Dish face*    A foreface in which there is a dip in the nasal bone so that the tip of the nose is higher than the stop, as in the Pointer.

*Docking*    Shortening a portion of the dog's tail by cutting.

*Domed skull*    See Apple-headed.

*Domino*    Reversal of the facial mask pattern on some breeds, such as the Afghan.

*Double coat*    Two types of coat on one dog. (See Topcoat and Undercoat.)

*Double handling*    Communication with an exhibit by another person from outside the ring (i.e. a person other than that handling the dog in the ring). A practice strictly against Kennel Club rules.

*Down-faced*    The opposite of dish-faced. The nasal bone inclines downwards from the stop to the top of the nose, as does that of the Bull Terrier.

*Down at pastern*  Having pasterns with a greater than desirable slope away from the perpendicular. A dog which is down at pastern tends to tire easily due to lack of tolerance to exercise. In a very few breeds, such as the Tibetan Terrier, slightly sloping pasterns are required.

*Drive*  Hindquarter propulsion. One often hears the term 'plenty of drive', indicating a dog with a powerful rear action.

*Drop-eared*  Having ears hanging down close and flat to the side of the skull, as in the Bloodhound. It can also be used to indicate a fault in a normally prick-eared breed, i.e. denoting that the ear is not fully erect.

*Dudley nose*  A brown or flesh-coloured nose, which is correct in some breeds. Also called putty nose.

*Ear carriage*  A combination of ear placement, position and use, creating an overall visual effect.

*East-West front*  Front feet which turn outwards rather than pointing straight forward.

*Ectropion*  Loose lower eyelids.

*Elbow*  The joint at the top of the fore arm. A dog which is 'out at elbow' or 'loose in elbow' means that the elbows drift away from the chest wall as the dog moves. This wastes energy and is a fault in the majority of breeds. 'Tied at elbow' or 'in at elbow' is the opposite, meaning that the elbows are too close to the chest wall, often such that the distance between the feet is greater than that between the elbows. This, too, is a fault. In a well-constructed dog the elbows should be well in but not so close as to restrict movement.

*Entire*  A male dog with two normal testes, fully descended into the scrotum, is said to be entire.

*Entropion*  Eyelids turn inwards causing the eyelash to contact the eyeball, thereby creating irritation.

*Ewe neck*  The top line of the neck is concave. An anatomical weakness.

*Faking*  Disguise of undesirable features by a method against Kennel Club rules.

*Fall*  The long fringe of hair which falls over the head of some breeds.

*Feathering*  Fine long fringes of hair at the back of the legs in breeds such as the English Setter. In some breeds the word can also refer to the longish coat on the ears, tail and belly. Fringing and plumage are other words used in this context, varying according to the breed.

*Felted*   Having a matted coat.

*Fiddle front*   Also commonly known as a Chippendale front, indicating that the elbows are wide apart, fore arms slope inwards and feet and pasterns turn out.

*Fiddle-headed*   Having an elongated, somewhat gaunt head with a pinched-in expression.

*Flag*   The tail of Setters and Retrievers.

*Flank*   Fleshy part of the side between the end of the ribs and the hip.

*Flecked*   Having a coat which is just lightly spotted with other colours but which is not roan or spotted, as in the English Setter.

*Flews*   Pendulous corners of the lips of the upper jaw.

*Floating ribs*   Those not connected with the sternum or cartilages of other ribs. Also known as false ribs.

*Flying ears*   An expression used for ears which tend to fly out in opposite directions or stand out further from the face than is expected for the breed. In gazehounds the term can be used to indicate the correct position of the ears when the dog is brought to attention.

*Fore arm*   The area from the elbow to the wrist.

*Foreface*   That area of the head from the ears to the tip of the nose.

*Forequarters*   The whole of the front assembly from the shoulders right down to the feet and including the fore legs, fore limbs and thoracic limbs.

*Free action*   Uninhibited free movement.

*Frill*   Long hair on front of neck and forechest.

*Frog face*   Used in connection with a dog such as the Bulldog when the nose extends too far forwards. Can also be used with reference to the expression of the Rottweiler due to the shape of the mouth.

*Frown*   Concerned expression caused by wrinkles above the eyes and across the head.

*Full eyes*   A term used to mean protruding, prominent eyes.

*Furnishings*   Abundance of coat on the extremities such as the head and tail.

*Furrow*   Groove running down the centre of the skull.

*Gait*   Movement or action.

*Gallop*   The fastest movement of the dog in which he is fully suspended in the air once during each sequence of the motion.

*Gay tail*   A tail which is carried up when it should not be.

*Gazehound*   A hound which hunts by sight rather than by smell.

*Giant breeds* Those which are much larger or heavier than the average.

*Grizzle* An iron-grey or bluish-grey colour.

*Guard hairs* The stiffer, usually longer hairs which serve as an outer jacket and protect the softer undercoat.

*Gun-barrel front* A front which is straight when viewed head on. Fore arms and pasterns are vertical to the ground and parallel.

*Hackney gait* Movement in which there is an exaggerated lift of the pasterns and front feet. The term is taken from the Hackney horse and while generally a fault it is correct in some breeds, such as the Miniature Pinscher.

*Hare foot* A long narrow foot, resembling that of the hare.

*Harlequin* Mottled or pied colour as in some Great Danes.

*Haunch bones* Hip bones.

*Haw* Pouching or sagging of the lower eyelid so that the inner surface of the lower eyelid shows. (See Ectropion).

*Head planes* Geometrical contours of the head from tip of nose to stop and from stop to occiput.

*Heart room* Indicating ample room inside the chest cavity to allow heart development and functions.

*Heat* A common term for a bitch's season or oestrus.

*Height* The height of a dog is measured from the withers to the ground when the dog is in a normal stance.

*Highly Commended* Sixth place.

*Hindquarters* The back assembly of the dog from the pelvic girdle down to the feet.

*Hip dysplasia* A developmental disease of the hip joint in which the head of the femur (thigh-bone) does not fit correctly into the socket of the pelvis.

*Hocks* The joint between the rear pastern and the lower thigh.

*Huckle bones* The top of the hip bones which can be seen above the back-line.

*In-breeding* The mating of closely related dogs such as father/daughter, mother/son, brother/sister.

*Incisors* A complete canine bite includes six incisors in both the upper and lower jaws. These are the teeth situated at the front of the mouth between the canines.

*Int. Ch.* International Champion.

*Irregular bite* A bite in which some of the incisor teeth are misplaced.

*Isabella* A straw-like fawn colour which can also be described as a light bay.

*Jowls*   Heavy, pendulous lips.

*Junior Warrant/JW*   A dog which has won a total of 25 Junior Warrant points between the ages of twelve and eighteen months will, upon application to the Kennel Club, be awarded a Junior Warrant. Points are allocated on the basis of three points for a first prize at a Championship show where Challenge Certificates are on offer for the breed, and one point for a first prize at an Open show or a Championship show without CCs for the breed. Points are awarded only for wins in breed competition.

*KCJO*   Kennel Club Junior Organisation.

*Keel*   The rounded curve of the brisket, as seen in the Dachshund.

*Kink tail*   A tail which is sharply bent, angled or broken somewhere along its length.

*Knee joint*   Stifle joint of the hind leg.

*Kneecap*   The patella, which is the small bone situated in a groove at the bottom of the thigh bone.

*Knitting*   Also commonly known as plaiting. Movement in which the legs cross over one another when the dog is in motion.

*Knuckling over*   Forward bend of the front leg at the wrist while the dog is standing. A weakness in the pastern joint.

*Layback*   A nose set back further than the chin in a breed such as the Bulldog is said to be laid back. Thus, when viewed in profile a straight line can be drawn from the forehead to the point of the chin.

*Layback of shoulder*   The degree of angulation of the shoulder blade.

*Leather*   The muscles and skin of the outer ear. This expression is used especially for Gundog breeds and the large hanging ears of some of the hounds.

*Leggy*   Too high on the leg (possibly as a result of being too short in the back). Can also be used to denote inadequate depth of chest in relation to the length of leg.

*Level back*   The height at withers is exactly the same as the height at the loins. This does not, however, indicate that the back is necessarily flat.

*Level bite*   A bite in which the edges of the upper and lower incisors meet edge to edge.

*Level top-line*   A term used to indicate that the line of the back is straight both when standing and when on the move. (The top-line itself is technically the entire upper outline when viewed in profile.)

*Line breeding*   The mating of dogs which are distantly or not too closely related, those having a common grandparent for example.

*Lippy*   Having excessively pendulous lips.

*Litter-mates*   Dogs which were born in the same litter.

*Liver*   A particular light brown colour which carries no trace of black pigmentation.

*Loaded shoulders*   Heavy, thick, muscular shoulders.

*Loin*   From the end of the rib-cage to the start of the pelvis, i.e. the upper part of the couplings.

*Lower thigh*   The region of muscle between the stifle and hock joints.

*Low set*   Indicating a short distance from the underline to the ground, especially in relation to the overall height at withers, such as in the Basset Hound and Dachshund.

*Lung room*   Dimensions of chest giving ample space for lung (and heart) development.

*Maiden bitch*   A bitch which has not been mated. (The Maiden class at shows has no connection with maiden used in this regard.)

*Mane*   Longish hair, usually of a coarser texture than the rest of the coat, which rises from the ridge of the neck and falls over the side. Also called a shawl.

*Mask*   Dark shading on the head forming a mask-like pattern.

*Merle*   A coat colouring of irregular dark blotches against a lighter background.

*Mis-marked*   Being coloured contrary to the requirements set down in the Breed Standard.

*Molars*   The two back teeth on either side of the top jaw and the three back teeth on either side of the bottom jaw.

*Molero*   A hole in the front of the centre of the skull which is covered only by the skin and hair. This a special feature of some Chihuahuas.

*Monorchid*   A male dog in which only one testicle has developed. (This term is frequently mistakenly used in relation to a unilateral cryptorchid.)

*Moustache*   Longish hair rising from the side of the face and lips, creating a moustache-like effect, as in the Deerhound.

*Moving close*   Can be applied to fore legs, hind legs or both when they are not well separated during movement.

*Muzzle*   The front portions of the upper and lower jaws between the stop and the tip of the nose.

*NAF*   Name applied for.

*NFC*   Not for competition.

*Occiput*   The prominent bone at the peak of the skull.

*Open coat*   Sparsely haired coat, often lacking in undercoat.

*Otter tail*   A thick, tapering tail which is densely coated with short, thick fur, as in the Labrador Retriever.

*Out of coat*   A term used to describe a dog which has for some reason, usually of a temporary nature, dropped its coat.

*Outcrossing*   Breeding from a dog and bitch which have no common ancestors, at least in the first five generations.

*Overbuilt*   Having excessive muscle development over the rump, giving the dog greater height in the hindquarters than in the fore hand.

*Overlay*   A mantle of dark shaded colour on a lighter background.

*Over-reaching*   The hind feet pass the front feet before making contact with the ground.

*Overshot*   The incisors of the upper jaw extend beyond those of the lower jaw so that no contact is made. Parrot mouth is also a term used to describe such a bite, especially if it is exceptionally overshot.

*Pacing*   Movement in which the two right feet move forward together followed by the two left ones. Some dogs tend to pace when walking at a slow speed.

*Pad*   The thickened portion of the sole of a dog's foot.

*Paddling*   Movement in which the front feet make a circular motion, flicking outwards at the end of each step.

*Paper feet*   Feet which have thin pads with a poor cushion.

*Particolour*   A coat of two colours, more or less equal in proportion. One of the two colours must be white.

*Pastern*   The area between the wrist and the foot.

*Pencilling*   Dark lines along the top of the toes of some breeds.

*Piebald*   Having irregular black body patches on a white background.

*Pied*   Having a coat of two colours in unequal proportions.

*Pigment*   Depth and intensity of colour and markings. Pigment is seen in eye rims, lips, eye colour, toenails, nose, etc.

*Pincer bite*   See Level bite.

*Pips*   Name used for spots above the eyes of some black and tan dogs.

*Plaiting*   See Knitting.

*Plume*   A tuft or fringe of long hair on the tail.

*Point of shoulder* The foremost point of the scapula (shoulder blade).

*Pot-hook tail* A tail carried above the back-line in an arc without touching the back.

*Prefix* See Affix.

*Premolars* The four teeth (sixteen in all) on each side of the top and bottom jaws, located behind the canines and in front of the molars.

*Prepotent* Exceptionally strong ability to reproduce certain qualities. The term tends to be used in connection with dogs rather than bitches.

*PRA* Progressive retinal atrophy. An inherited form of blindness.

*Prick ears* Stiff, upstanding ears. Also known as erect ears.

*Putty nose.* See Dudley nose.

*Quarters* In canine terminology 'quarters' often denotes the pelvic and thigh regions.

*Racy* Slight in build and long in leg, like the Whippet or Greyhound. Can be used to describe an individual part of the body such as the hindquarters.

*Rangy* Tall and long in the body; frequently light in frame.

*Reach* The distance covered by each stride when in motion.

*Reverse scissor bite* The teeth of the lower jaw extending beyond those of the upper jaw, so that the front of the top teeth meet with the back of the bottom ones.

*Reserve* Fourth place in a class.

*Reserve Challenge Certificate/Res CC/RCC* Reserve to the Challenge Certificate winner.

*Ribbed-up* Having ribs extending back along the body.

*Ring tail* A long tail, all or part of which curves or curls. A fault in many breeds but correct in some, such as the Afghan.

*Roach* A roached back is arched convexly along the spine. The term is commonly used in relation to a roach towards the hindquarters, but strictly speaking a simple roach can be anywhere along the back except over the loin. If the roach does extend as far as the tail it is more correctly termed a wheel back.

*Roan* A uniform mixture of coloured and white hairs.

*Rolling gait* Characteristic rolling motion of the Pekingese caused by the shape of the rib-cage.

*Root* Base of tail.

*Rudder* A term used for the tail of water dogs in particular.

*Ruff*   Thick long hair around the whole of the neck area; often coarsely textured.

*Run on*   To retain a puppy in the hope that it will turn out well enough for the purpose one has in mind, usually the show-ring.

*Runt*   Usually used in connection with young puppies. Small, weedy, weak or stunted specimen of a breed.

*Sable*   A colour produced by black-tipped hairs on a background of another colour; termed gold sable, silver sable, grey sable, etc.

*Saddle*   Short hair pattern along the back of an Afghan Hound, or a solid area of colour on the shoulder and back.

*Scissor bite*   Upper incisors closely overlap the lower ones, so that the inside of the top teeth touch the outside of the bottom ones.

*Scrambled mouth*   Teeth not all set in a straight line, often seen in a narrow jaw. Also called a jumbled mouth.

*Screw tail*   A short tail which is twisted, kinked or can be a spiral.

*Scrotum*   The scrotal sac containing the two testicles in an entire male.

*Second mouth*   The second set of teeth, i.e. the permanent set which replaces the milk teeth.

*Self coloured*   Of one solid colour all over.

*Self marked*   Of solid colour with white or pale markings on chest, feet and tip of tail.

*Set on*   Term used to describe the place at which the ear meets the skull and that at which the tail meets the rump.

*Shawl*   See Mane/Ruff.

*Shelly*   Having a narrow, somewhat weedy body.

*Shelly bone*   Porous thin bone which is lacking in strength.

*Shoulder*   Used as a general term to cover the whole of the top section of the fore leg, from the withers down to the elbow.

*Show Champion/Sh. Ch.*   Any Gundog or Border Collie awarded three Challenge Certificates under three different judges, at least one of the CCs having been awarded after the dog is twelve months of age.

*Sickle-hocked*   Refers to the shape and contours of the components of the hock joint. If the pastern slopes it lessens the angle of the hock joint. In profile the lower thigh and hind pastern form the shape of a sickle.

*Sight hound*   See Gazehound.

*Single coat*   Many breeds have an outer coat and an undercoat and are thus 'double-coated'. A single-coated dog has only one coat, like the Italian Greyhound or Pointer.

*Single tracking* Convergence of the pads to a central line when in motion. A natural movement for the longer-legged breeds. In shorter-legged breeds there is less convergence due to the general body structure.

*Slab-sided* Having ribs that are not well sprung; a fault in most breeds. (See Spring of rib.)

*Slack back* See Sway back, of which a slack back is a mild form, due usually to a structural weakness.

*Snipy* A pointed, weak muzzle which is too long and too narrow.

*Socks* Markings resembling white socks on the feet and pasterns of a dark-coloured animal.

*Soundness* Quality of a dog which is well constructed throughout. A dog can also be described as being sound in temperament.

*Spectacles* The light-coloured area around the eyes on a dark-headed dog.

*Spaying* A bitch which has had surgery preventing her from having puppies is said to have been spayed.

*Splay feet* Toes set far apart from one another, irrespective of foot shape. This term is generally used to describe a defect but is desirable in a very few breeds such as the Irish Water Spaniel.

*Spotted* Can mean speckled, flecked or ticked.

*Spring of rib* The shape of the ribs as they emerge from the vertebral column. A dog with a good spring of rib can also be said to be well sprung, well arched, or well rounded.

*Square* A dog in which the measurement from point of shoulder to point of buttock is roughly equal to that from withers to ground. A requirement in certain breeds.

*Stand-off coat* Hair standing out from the body as opposed to lying flat to the skin. Usually longish, heavy and harsh in texture and frequently supported by a soft, dense undercoat.

*Steep* Used to indicate insufficient angulation, especially in relation to the shoulder and upper arm.

*Stifle* The knee joint between the upper and lower thighs.

*Stockings* White hair covering most of the leg on a dog which is otherwise primarily of a dark colour.

*Stools* Faeces.

*Stop* The depression in the top-line of the head almost centrally between the eyes. A steep or deep stop is clearly in evidence on the short-faced breeds.

*Stud dog* A male dog which is used to mate bitches.

*Substance* Generally used with reference to bone being well developed, indicating both strength and density of bone.

*Suffix*   An affix used at the end of a dog's name.

*Sway back*   A back which sags somewhere along its length. The sag may vary according to degree and position. This can also be termed a dippy/hollow/saddle/slack/soft or swampy back.

*TAF*   Transfer applied for

*Tail carriage*   The manner in which the tail is carried.

*Team*   Three or more exhibits. Can be of either sex or mixed but must belong to the same exhibitor.

*Terrier front*   Considered a virtue or a fault according to the breed. A Terrier front is one in which the front is moderately wide and in which the fore arms are parallel to one another from chest to ground.

*Thick skull*   A coarse skull, indicating excessive width due to thick, coarse bone.

*Third eyelid*   Located in the inner corner of the eye is the third eyelid which is a membrane used by the dog as a protective device. It is generally pink in colour but in most cases the outer rim is pigmented so that it is not noticeable at first glance. If the outer rim is not pigmented it can clearly be seen when the eye is open.

*Throatiness*   Too much loose skin around the throat.

*Thumb marks*   Black or dark-coloured marks in different places on the coat according to the breed.

*Tickling*   Small dark flecks of colour, usually on a white background colour.

*Tie*   The locking together of a dog and bitch during mating.

*Tied at elbow*   See Elbow.

*Timber*   A term used to denote bones, usually those of the legs.

*Toeing-in*   Fore feet rotate in towards each other rather than being directly in line with the pastern. This term can be used for dogs standing or on the move.

*Topknot*   Tuft of long hair on the head of some breeds, such as the Afghan, Shih Tzu and Bedlington Terrier. The texture of the topknot varies according to the breed.

*Top-line*   See Level top-line.

*Trace*   A dark mark down the back of a Pug.

*Tri-colour*   A coat of three colours which are usually black, tan and white but can also be blue, roan and tan or liver, white and tan.

*Trousers*   Long or longish hair at the back of the legs of some breeds.

*True front*   Straight front.

*True movement*   Indicates that the feet and legs move in correct alignment.

*Tuck-up*   The underline of the abdomen as it sweeps up towards the flank or hindquarters.

*Tucked up*   An expression used for a dog which is not looking well. (Not to be confused with Tuck-up.)

*Tulip ears*   Stiffly upright ears with edges curved slightly forward to resemble a tulip petal. Correct in some breeds but a fault in others.

*Type/Typey*   Has the quality of conforming to the Breed standard.

*Umbrella*   A cap-like fall of hair over the eyes, as in the Hungarian Puli and Old English Sheepdog.

*Undercoat*   Soft, often dense hair under the longer outer hair on some breeds.

*Undershot*   Having lower incisor teeth protruding beyond the upper incisors so that they do not meet each other, as in the Bulldog. Can also be described as underhung.

*Unsound*   The opposite of sound. A dog which, be it for physical or mental reasons, is incapable of carrying out the functional role of the breed.

*Upper arm*   The humerus bone of the forequarters, i.e. the bone below the scapula.

*Upper thigh*   The area between the hip joint and the stifle. Also known as the shank.

*Upright in shoulder*   As steep in shoulder.

*Uterus*   The womb.

*Vagina*   The genital passage of a bitch.

*Veil*   Long hair falling down over the eyes, as in the Skye Terrier.

*Vent*   Generally used in reference to the tan colour under the tail of some breeds, but can mean the area around the anus (including the vulva in a bitch).

*Vulva*   External portion of the vagina.

*Very Highly Commended/VHC*   Fifth place.

*Waist*   A clearly defined narrowing of the body over the loins, especially in comparison with width of chest.

*Wall eye*   Eyes which appear white and blue (due to incomplete distribution of melanin deposits), as seen in breeds carrying the merle colour such as the Collie, Cardigan and Welsh Corgis, etc. Can also be know as china/fish/jewelled/marbled or silver eye.

*Weaving*   See Plaiting.

*Weedy*   Too lightly framed with inadequate bone. Can imply that the dog is stunted in development or has not thrived well. Lacking in substance.

*Well knit*   Denoting that the sections of the body are firmly joined. Also used as a synonym for short coupled. (See Coupling.)

*Well ribbed up*   Ribcage extending well back along the body.

*Well sprung*   See Spring of rib.

*Wheaten*   Peal yellow colour found in some Terrier breeds. Can also be called straw.

*Wheel back*   See Roach back.

*Whelp*   A puppy from time of birth until it is weaned.

*Whelping*   The act of a bitch giving birth to her puppies (or whelps).

*Whiskers*   Hair rising from the chin, side of face or both. This is often strong, thick and harsh but can be soft in some breeds.

*Widow's peak*   Triangular shape in the coat markings of the forehead, most usually seen on sable and bi-coloured dogs.

*Winter nose*   A nose which is poorly pigmented, strictly speaking in the winter months.

*Wire-haired*   Having a harsh, crisp, dense coat, used primarily in relation to the rough-haired terriers. See also Broken coat.

*Withers*   The region of union between the upper portion of the shoulder blades and the first and second thoracic vertebrae. Seen as the junction behind the base of the neck and the back. It is from this point that the height of a dog is measured.

*Wrinkle*   Loose folds of skin, primarily on the head and neck but otherwise anywhere on the body, as in the Shar-Pei.

*Wry mouth*   The lower jaw is twisted to one side so that the upper and lower jaws are out of alignment with one another.

*Zygomatic arch*   The bony ridge which forms the lower border of the eye socket.

# A short glossary of show-goers' colloquialisms

*Big Green One*   Challenge Certificate.

*Bridesmaid*   A term used typically to describe a bitch which seems always to be awarded Reserve Challenge Certificates rather than Challenge Certificates. Can also be used in relation to one which frequently comes second but rarely wins.

*Can't get past*   It is often said that one 'can't get past' such-and-such a dog, meaning that it is almost impossible to beat him.

*Down the line*   Not placed first or second; used especially with reference to Reserve or VHC placings.

*Facey/face judging*   Appearing to be judging people rather than dogs, i.e. placing those exhibitors who have well-known faces. (Do always keep in mind that often the well-known faces have very good dogs!)

*Gained his crown/title*   Became a Champion.

*Go over*   A judge 'goes over' a dog to assess his attributes; the actual placing of the hands on the dog's body for the purpose of assessment.

*Good doer*   A dog which eats and thrives well.

*In the cards*   Awarded one of the prizes in a class.

*In good company*   Used to indicate that although one's dog was not placed there were other good dogs which were also not awarded a placing.

*Judging the other end of the lead*   Judging the handler rather than the dog.

*Knocked*   Put down to a lower place than might have been expected.

*Laying on of hands*   Said of a judge who goes through the motions of going over a dog, but apparently does not feel the dog well enough to assess structure.

*Looking for his third*   Hoping to win a third Challenge Certificate and therefore be made a Champion.

*Made up*   Became a Champion.

*New dog*   A dog which has not been seen in a previous class by a judge who is officiating.

*Pulled out*   Selected in the final few for the placings in a class. 'Pulled out but not placed' is commonly used to indicate that the judge did consider the dog further but then did not place him.

*Put through*   Generally used at Championship level to indicate the dog which has been declared Best of Breed and has therefore been 'put through' to the Group.

*Put up*   Placed first. Can also be used in relation to the winner of a Challenge Certificate.

*Reserve Ticket*   Reserve Challenge Certificate.

*Seen dog*   A dog which has been entered in a second or subsequent class under the same judge (even if the judge assessed the dog for the first time in a breed class and secondly in an Any Variety class, or vice versa).

*Set up*   To present one's dog in a standing position for the judge.

*Stack/stacked*   Has the same meaning as set up.

*Table dog*   One which is examined by a judge on the table rather than on the floor.

*Thrown out*   Not placed. 'Thrown out with the rubbish' is also frequently heard.

*Ticket*   Challenge Certificate.

# A few major do's and don'ts

DO   post your entries on time, using first-class mail.

DO   pack the car the night before a show.

DO   arrive in good time for judging.

DO   give your dog plenty of praise, win or lose.

DO   offer your dog water at regular intervals throughout the day.

DO   give your dog the chance to relieve himself at frequent intervals.

DO   congratulate the winner of your class if your own dog comes second or third.

DO   clean up after your dog.

DO   select your clothes carefully to complement your dog.

DO   wear the correct ring number.

DO   know the age of your dog.

DO   keep an eye on the judge at all times.

DO   compete for Best in Group and, if applicable, Best in Show if your dog has been awarded Best of Breed.


DON'T   leave your dog unattended on a bench for long periods.

DON'T   spread gossip or rumours.

DON'T   be a bad loser.

DON'T   begin a long conversation with the judge in the ring.

DON'T   wear clompy shoes.

DON'T   jangle money or keys in your pocket.

DON'T   have your dog's benching chain too long.

DON'T   leave your dog in a car unless the weather is cool, and even then he must be checked frequently.

DON'T   allow your dog to be a nuisance to other dogs.

DON'T   inadvertently tread on another exhibitor's dog.

DON'T   wear rosettes in the ring except in the Group or Best in Show ring.

DON'T    tear up a prize card in the ring, however disappointed you may be.

DON'T    refuse to challenge for an award if invited to do so.

DON'T    treat your dog unkindly in the ring (or out of it).

DON'T    allow the lead to dangle down, especially when moving your dog.

DON'T    put yourself between your dog and the judge when moving your exhibit.

DON'T    give up too soon – there's always another day and another judge!

*Despite what some non-showgoers think, most dogs enjoy being on their benches. And if Mum's left her shoes behind she* must *be coming back!*

# Useful Addresses

The Kennel Club
1–5 Clarges Street
Piccadilly
London
W1Y 8AB
Tel: 071-493 6651

*Our Dogs* Publishing Company Limited
5 Oxford Road Station Approach
Manchester
M60 1SX
Tel: (061) 236 2660

*Dog World* Limited
9 Tufton Street
Ashford
Kent
TN23 1QN
Tel: (0233) 621877

# Selected Bibliography

Compton, Herbert, *The Twentieth Century Dog*, Grant Richards, 1904.

Harmer, Hilary, *Showing and Judging Dogs*, John Gifford, 1977.

Horner, Tom, *Take Them Round Please – The Art of Judging Dogs* David & Charles, 1975.

Hutchinson, W. (ed.), *Hutchinson's Popular Illustrated Dog Encyclopaedia*, 1933–4.

Lane, C.H, *Dog Shows and Doggy People*, Hutchinson & Co., 1902.

Leighton, Robert, *The New Book of the Dog*, Cassell and Co, 1907.

McDowell Lyon, *The Dog in Action*, Howell Book House Inc., 1978.

Page Elliot, Rachel, *Dogsteps – Illustrated Gait at a Glance*, Howell Book House Inc., 1973.

Spira, Harold R., *Canine Terminology*, Harper & Row (Australasia) Pty Ltd, 1982.

Vesey-FitzGerald, Brian, *The Domestic Dog*, Routledge & Kegan Paul Ltd, 1957.

# Index